GAIL DUFF

MICROWAVE COOKERY

HAMLYN

NOTE

1. Metric and imperial measurements have been calculated separately. Use one set of measurements only as they are not exact equivalents.

2. All spoon measures are level unless otherwise stated.

3. All recipes serve 4 unless otherwise stated.

Acknowledgements

We would like to thank: **Valerie Clarke; Jennifer Hudson; Chris Laing; Paul Gregory, Microwave Ovenware Ltd.,** Teddington, Middlesex; **Trevor Hamer, Philips Electrical,** Philips Major Appliances, Lightcliffe, Halifax; **Mr C. Crocker, Deeko Ltd.,** Garman Road, London N17; **Mrs Michelle Kershaw, Lakeland Plastics,** Alexandra Buildings, Station Precinct, Windermere, Cumbria; **Boots Cookshops** and **Boots Houseware Departments; Poole Pottery,** c/o Munro-Deighton Public Relations Ltd., 28 Newman Street, London W1; **Brian Cook and Son,** Charing, Kent; **Frank Hogben and Son,** Charing, Kent; **Lurcocks of Lenham,** Lenham, Maidstone, Kent; **Mick Clarke, Honesty Wholefoods,** Union Street, Maidstone, Kent.

Produced by New Leaf Productions

Photography by Mick Duff
Design by Jim Wire
Series Editor: Sarah Wallace

First published in 1984 by Hamlyn Publishing
Bridge House, London Road,
Twickenham, Middlesex, England

Sixth impression 1986

ISBN 0 600 20808 7

Printed in Spain

D. L. TF. 643-1984

CONTENTS

INTRODUCTION

Microwave cookers are fast becoming a standard feature in an increasing number of homes and it will not be long before they are as popular as the freezer.

A microwave cooker is not only an oven. It can perform numerous tasks including casseroling, steaming, roasting, melting, reheating and thawing, all in a matter of minutes. Owning such an appliance will open up a new and exciting aspect of cooking, but as it is so different from cooking with a conventional oven, the first step is to find out how a microwave oven works and how to use it to its best advantage.

What is a microwave cooker?

A microwave cooker consists of a basic unit which is usually smaller than a conventional oven, the average capacity being 0.9 cu ft. or its metric equivalent. It can be plugged into an ordinary 13 or 15 amp socket and has controls which basically consist of an on/off switch and timer.

When the cooker is switched on, the ordinary domestic electricity supply is increased by a built-in power transformer. The resulting higher voltage electrical energy is then converted into electro-magnetic or microwave energy which is directed towards the oven cavity by a waveguide. A fan, sometimes referred to as the paddle or wave stirrer, is fitted in the top of the oven and this slowly turns to aid the even distribution of the waves. The oven is lined with metal which reflects the waves onto the food.

All models have a tight-fitting door with a built-in cut-out device which automatically switches off the cooker as soon as the door is opened. This door is often made of glass so that the food can be seen, but is reinforced by a metal mesh so that the energy cannot pass through it.

How does a microwave cooker work?

Microwaves are electro-magnetic waves which transmit energy through space, and a microwave cooker makes use of this energy in exactly the same way as a television or radio. Microwaves are short waves, hence their name. They are reflected off metal and so when they enter the metal-lined cooker they move around creating an energy pattern. The waves can pass through other material such as china, glass, paper, wood and some plastics, but are absorbed by water particles in food. They cause the water particles to twist backwards and forwards at over two thousand million times a second, generating heat by friction.

The microwaves are absorbed extremely quickly by the food, but as they are short they only penetrate to a depth of 4–5cm/1½–2in. You can, however, cook food thicker than this, such as large joints of meat or cakes, as the heat carries on through the food by conduction. The whole cooking process will still be far shorter than if you were using a conventional oven.

Types of microwave cooker
The most popular type of microwave cooker is the small one which will fit on a worktop or sturdy shelf, can be fitted into kitchen units or onto a special trolley.

Double oven microwave cookers consist of a microwave cooker built into the same unit as a large conventional oven. You can also buy a combined unit which consists of a free-standing cooker with a hob, conventional oven and eye-level microwave.

Standard features
All microwave cookers have an on/off switch which usually starts the fan and the interior light. The microwave energy is switched on by a further switch or button. There is a timer which enables you to time cooking to the nearest 15 seconds and a bell or buzzer which indicates when the cooking time has elapsed. At this point the oven will automatically switch off.

Additional features
Most microwave cookers now have a variable power control which enables you to cook on a high or low heat. Some simply have two settings; others may have high, medium and low settings, numbered settings from 1–10 or settings indicated by the names of cooking processes, such as roast, simmer or reheat. It is best to choose a microwave cooker with variable controls.

Another essential control to look for is the defrost switch. When operated it will pulse the microwave energy on and off so that the heat spreads slowly through the food, which will then become evenly thawed. If a cooker does not have such a control, the energy must be manually turned on and off. If a cooker does not have a variable power control but does have a defrost switch, the defrost setting can be used for slow cooking.

Some of the more recent models of microwave oven have touch button controls and a slot to take pre-programmed recipe cards. Others have a memory bank which is capable of storing 2 or more cooking programmes.

The microwaves within any cooker may not be evenly distributed. To overcome this problem and make sure that the food cooks evenly, some cookers have a built-in turntable which operates all the time when the oven is switched on. The only disadvantage of this is that you cannot use large oblong or oval food containers in the cooker. Other types of cooker have a rotating antenna system which moves the microwaves around the food to ensure even cooking. If a microwave cooker does not have either of these facilities, the food should be turned round manually several times during cooking.

Food does not readily brown in a microwave. In some cases a special browning dish is supplied with the oven, but if not, this can be bought separately. There are also a few models of cooker that have a built-in browning element which operates rather like a conventional grill and which should be used either before or after the cooking process. If neither of these facilities is available, food can be browned quickly under a conventional grill after cooking.

One of the newest types of microwave cooker combines microwave cooking with convection cooking and this means that you can have the advantage of both microwave speed and conventional oven browning facilities.

If you have a large family you might find a 2-level microwave cooker an advantage. This has a shelf which enables you to cook 2 dishes at once.

A temperature probe is another extra provided by some manufacturers. It is inserted into the joint of roasting meat and, when the meat reaches the temperature required to complete the cooking, the probe will automatically switch off the oven. If a probe is not provided you can insert a special microwave oven thermometer into the roasting meat and keep a check on the temperature yourself; or you can use an ordinary meat thermometer, provided you only use it as a check after the meat has come out of the oven.

Is microwave cooking safe?
Yes, it is extremely safe. The microwaves that cook the food are what is known as non-ionizing which means that they cannot damage body cells. They only create heat which has no more effect on the body than normal heat. What is more, these waves are contained in the microwave oven by the electrically sealed door which has up to 6 interlocking safety switches. As soon as the door is opened the power goes off and it will not come on again until the door is closed.

In special testing laboratories, microwave doors are opened a hundred thousand times and measurements are taken for leakages every ten thousand times. The interlocks are also tested and it has been proved that if one of the interlocks fails, the door seal will still remain effective. These tests are the equivalent of using the microwave seven times a day for almost 40 years.

Microwave cooking can actually be safer than

cooking with a conventional oven and hob. There are no saucepans to boil over and there is no danger of being burned on an oven or hot plate.

It is worth remembering that there is no evidence that anyone has ever been harmed by a microwave cooker.

What are the advantages of microwave cooking?

The advantages of microwave cooking are many. A microwave cooker can be installed in any room with no special plug or fittings. You can cook a dish in minutes and produce a number of dishes in a relatively short time. It is very easy to cook small quantities and therefore a microwave is ideal if you have to cook separate meals for small children or those on special diets.

Fewer saucepans and containers are required than when using a conventional oven and there is less danger of burning yourself. This makes a microwave cooker ideal for family use and for use by the disabled. It also reduces the amount of washing-up.

The cooker itself is extremely easy to clean and however long you cook with it there will be no condensation or smell in the kitchen.

The costs of running a microwave cooker are low. All the energy is concentrated on the food. None is wasted on the pans or on a heating-up time.

Microwave cooking is extremely healthy. The short cooking time and the relatively small amount of water needed cuts down on vitamin loss.

Food can be reheated quickly in a microwave without it drying up or spoiling. Frozen foods, whether raw or cooked, can be defrosted quickly and safely.

What can a microwave cooker do?

Most cooking processes can be carried out very successfully in a microwave oven. You can soften butter and melt ingredients such as chocolate or gelatine. You can make soups and sauces; heat hot drinks; cook fish; roast meat and poultry; bake eggs and make omelettes; cook vegetables; bake cakes, bread and puddings; blanch almonds and toast coconut; make preserves in small quantities; reheat dishes and thaw frozen foods.

Are there any limitations?

Just a few. Never cook eggs in their shells in any microwave oven as they will explode. Also, never deep or shallow fry as the fat will splatter.

Flaky, rough puff and choux pastries cannot be cooked successfully and neither can Yorkshire puddings, roast potatoes, soufflés, some types of bread and cakes, and pancakes.

If you have a microwave combined with a fan oven, these baking techniques are possible, but pancakes can still only be cooked on a hob.

The microwave's ability to brown meats is limited unless there is a built-in browning element or, again, you have a combination of microwave and fan oven. Grilling is not successful in any microwave oven without a browning element.

Ideally a microwave cooker should be used in conjunction with a conventional oven and hob. This way you will get the best from both and cooking will be a pleasure.

What cookware should be used in a microwave oven?

The golden rule when cooking in a microwave oven is never to use metal containers. This includes not only the usual range of roasting, cake and flan tins, but also any china or glass that has a metal decoration, or glassware made from lead crystal. Microwaves are reflected off metal and if a metal container were used, the waves would not be able to penetrate the food. There would also be a danger of damaging the cooker.

All types of china can be used in a microwave oven. Dishes are useful for complete meals and plates can be used to hold food for reheating or as a cover. Round straight-sided soufflé dishes are useful for baking. Drinks can be made in cups, and sauces and custards in jugs.

Some pottery and earthenware can be used, but these tend to be porous and contain moisture. They therefore take microwaves away from the food, thus lengthening the cooking time. They also get hot and difficult to handle.

Microwaves do not affect glass, but the temperature of the food might cause it to break so always make sure that it is of a fairly sturdy type. You can warm milk drinks and hot toddies in glasses, bake in straight-sided glass dishes and bake grapefruit in small round dishes. You can also convert a straight-sided dish into a ring mould by placing a jam jar in the centre.

Many special plastic containers are now made for use in microwave ovens and they are the ideal cookware to use. They never detract energy from the food, they are light and easy to handle and easy to clean. They come in varying shapes and sizes and will suit every purpose. If other types of plastic container are used, try the 'container test' explained below to make sure that they are able to withstand the temperature that the food reaches.

Cardboard can be put into a microwave oven. There are several ranges of 'ovenable' cardboard containers available. You can also line other types of cardboard cups and boxes with cling-film or greaseproof paper and use them for baking.

Kitchen paper absorbs moisture and fat; use it to wrap round pastry and bread for reheating and also for covering bacon and other foods that might splatter.

Food can be wrapped in greaseproof or parchment paper for cooking in a microwave, but never use waxed paper as the wax will melt and spoil the food.

Bread rolls can be wrapped in linen or cotton napkins for quick heating in a microwave oven. Be careful with basketware and wood. They can be used safely but will dry out and crack if they are put into the oven too often or for too long a period.

Roasting bags are ideal for cooking joints of meat and vegetables. Cling-film is invaluable for covering many foods. The type made specially for use in a microwave oven is stronger and better than that normally used only for wrapping. Always pierce the cling-film to let out excess steam. Foods in boil-in-the-bag pouches can be put directly into the microwave oven once the bags have been pierced.

If you are not sure whether your dish is suitable for cooking in a microwave oven, try the container test. Put a cup of water into the oven next to the container that you are testing. Microwave on high for $1\frac{1}{4}$ minutes. The water should be hot and the container cool. If the container is hot and the water cool, the container is not suitable. If both are warm, use the container for short cooking periods only.

Choose a container that fits the food. For example, fish should be spread out in a wide, shallow container and milk should be heated in a tall jug as it may boil over. Use round containers or those with rounded corners. Sharp corners attract the heat and cause overcooking in those areas.

Basic microwave cooking techniques

Timing The timing is all-important when cooking in a microwave oven. It depends on quantity, starting temperature and the type of food to be cooked.

The more food you put into a microwave oven, the longer the cooking time will be. Generally, if you double the amount of food in a given recipe you must increase the cooking time by between one-third and one-half again. When halving the amount of food, the cooking time should be just over half the original.

Food coming directly out of the refrigerator will take longer to cook than food at room temperature. You may even find that some foods take slightly longer to cook on a very cold day.

Lighter textured food will cook and reheat faster than something more dense – for example, bread takes less time than a piece of meat of the same weight.

Fat and sugar in foods attract more heat but the more water that you add to foods, the longer they will take to cook as the water will absorb the heat.

Size and shape of foods Thicker foods take longer to cook than thin slices or foods that are chopped, so a joint of meat will take longer to cook than a casserole containing the same weight of diced meat. When you are cooking a casserole, make sure that all the ingredients are chopped to the same size for even cooking.

If you have an odd-shaped piece of meat such as a leg of lamb, or a whole chicken, cover the thinner parts such as the wing tips or end of the leg with aluminium foil to prevent overcooking in these areas.

Arranging food To ensure an even distribution of the microwaves, food should be evenly placed on the cooking dish preferably with space around it. Ideally, it should be arranged around the outside of a round dish with a space in the middle. If food is of an irregular shape, put it with the thicker, denser parts towards the outside of the dish. Vegetables should be put into the dish in an even layer.

Covering food Covering food with a lid or cling-film retains steam and moisture, speeding up the cooking process and helping meat to tenderize. Foods that you wish to keep dry such as bread or pastry should be covered with kitchen paper to absorb moisture.

Stirring and turning food The microwaves penetrate the outer edges of the food first, heating them up before the centre. Foods such as sauces and soups should be stirred regularly during the cooking time and vegetables and casseroles should be turned in the dish. Large joints of meat should be turned over at least once. If a microwave oven has no built-in turntable or roving antenna system, the cooking dish should be turned through a 90° or 180° angle at least once during cooking.

Standing time After the microwave oven has been switched off, the food continues to cook by conduction of heat towards the centre. This heat will complete the cooking process.

The length of standing time necessary will depend on the volume and density of the food. With large joints of meat, poultry and some baked foods it can be up to 20 minutes and with these types of foods it must always be observed. When testing for readiness, always slightly undercook and then test after the standing time.

Reheating When reheating a complete dish, turn the oven on for a short time and allow a period of standing time. This will ensure that the food does not overcook. When reheating a meal on a plate, keep the heights of the food even and arrange the more densely textured foods around the outside of the plate. Slices of meat should be covered with gravy or stock to prevent them from drying.

Thawing When food is frozen, ice crystals form within it. When defrosting takes place in a microwave oven, the waves are attracted to these crystals and the areas around them thaw out quickly. If the frozen food is subjected to the full power of the oven for a long period the final result would be food that is partly cooked, partly thawed and partly still frozen. If the oven is continually switched on and off, the heat created while it is on will gradually spread during the resting period so that the food is evenly thawed.

Most microwave ovens have a defrost setting which automatically switches the oven on and off. Where one is not fitted, use a low setting and turn it on and off at regular intervals.

Always thaw food such as casseroles or soups in a container which fits the food. The thawed liquid will then remain close to the block and so conduct the heat through to the part that is still frozen.

Care of your microwave cooker

Microwave ovens are easy to keep clean and need only be wiped with a damp cloth after each use. Never use scouring pads or powder, aerosol sprays or caustic cleaners, as these may scratch the metal lining and cause the production of small sparks when the oven is next used.

Should smells build up inside the oven, place a cup or bowl inside containing 3 parts water to 1 part lemon juice and cook on high for 10 minutes.

The door seals are important, so never let food accumulate around them. Do not let children tamper with the seals and make sure that the door is never knocked or leant on. The switches and controls should never be tampered with.

The oven should not be operated without food inside as this could damage it. It is therefore a good idea to keep a cup or glass of water in the oven in case it is accidentally switched on.

If the oven is used frequently it is a good idea to have it serviced every 12 months by the manufacturer.

SOUPS AND STARTERS

Soups can be made quickly and conveniently in a microwave oven and the basic stock which gives them so much natural flavour can be made in less than half the time that it takes on a conventional hob.

Small but delicious starters can be prepared, cooked and on the table in minutes.

BASIC STOCK

1 set chicken giblets or 1 small beef marrow bone
1 onion, halved, not peeled
1 carrot, roughly chopped
1 celery stick, roughly chopped
bouquet garni
1 bayleaf
1 tsp black peppercorns

Put all the ingredients into a large bowl. Fill the bowl with water. Cover and microwave on high for 30 minutes. Leave to stand for 20 minutes and strain.

Store the stock in a covered plastic container in the refrigerator for up to 5 days.

BORTSCH

350g/12 oz beetroot
225g/8 oz carrots
6 celery sticks
1 large onion
900ml/1½ pints ham stock
1 garlic clove, crushed with a pinch of salt
150ml/¼ pint soured cream

Cut the vegetables into matchstick pieces. Put the vegetables into a bowl with 150ml/¼ pint of the stock. Cover and microwave on high for 20 minutes, stirring halfway through.

Pour in the remaining stock and add the garlic. Microwave on high, uncovered, for 15 minutes. Serve in individual bowls, topped with soured cream.

MUSHROOM AND RED WINE SOUP

225g/8 oz dark, flat mushrooms
25g/1 oz butter
1 large onion, finely chopped
2 tbsp flour
750ml/1¼ pints stock
1 bayleaf
150ml/¼ pint dry red wine
6 tbsp chopped parsley

Finely chop the mushrooms. Put the butter and onion into a dish. Cover with cling-film or a lid and microwave on high for 3 minutes. Stir in the mushrooms, cover again and microwave on high for 2 minutes.

Stir in the flour and stock. Add the bayleaf. Microwave on high, uncovered, for 5 minutes.

Pour in the wine, add the parsley and microwave on high for 2 minutes. Discard the bayleaf before serving.

TOMATO AND ORANGE SOUP

450g/1 lb tomatoes
1 large onion, finely chopped
1 garlic clove, finely chopped
25g/1 oz butter
1 tsp dried mixed herbs
grated rind and juice of 1 large orange
2 tbsp tomato purée
600ml/1 pint stock
4 tbsp sherry

Scald, skin and finely chop the tomatoes. Put the onion and garlic into a bowl with the butter. Cover with cling-film or a lid and microwave on high for 4 minutes.

Add the tomatoes and herbs, cover again and microwave on high for 10 minutes so the tomatoes are soft. Stir in the orange rind and juice, tomato purée and stock. Microwave on high for 10 minutes. Add the sherry just before serving.

CREAM OF CARROT SOUP

450g/1 lb carrots
1 large onion
25g/1 oz butter
900ml/1½ pints stock
salt and pepper
bouquet garni
150ml/¼ pint soured cream
1 garlic clove, crushed with a pinch of salt

Thinly slice the carrots and onion and put the sliced vegetables into a dish with the butter and 4 tbsp of stock. Cover with a lid or with cling-film.

Microwave on high for 10 minutes. Pour in the rest of the stock. Season and add the bouquet garni. Microwave on high, uncovered, for 15 minutes. Remove the bouquet garni.

Work the soup in a blender or food processor until smooth. Add the soured cream and garlic and blend again. Alternatively, put the soup through the fine blade of a vegetable mill, mix a little with the soured cream and garlic and stir the mixture into the rest of the soup.

Return the soup to the cooking dish and microwave on high for 2–3 minutes or until heated through.

CELERY AND STILTON SOUP

6 celery sticks
25g/1 oz butter
1 large onion, finely chopped
2 tbsp flour
900ml/1½ pints stock
bouquet garni
100g/4 oz grated Stilton cheese

Finely chop the celery and put into a bowl with the butter and onion. Cover with cling-film or a lid and microwave on high for 10 minutes. Stir in the flour and stock and add the bouquet garni. Microwave on high, uncovered, for 10 minutes. Remove the bouquet garni.

Put the cheese into a bowl and gradually stir in 150ml/¼ pint of the soup. Stir the mixture back into the rest of the soup. Microwave on high, uncovered, for 2 minutes.

ARTICHOKE AND TOMATO SOUP

450g/1 lb Jerusalem artichokes
1 large onion, thinly sliced
25g/1 oz butter
450g/1 lb tomatoes
600ml/1 pint stock
bouquet garni
salt and freshly ground black pepper

Peel the artichokes and drop them immediately into cold water to which you have added a dash of vinegar. Thinly slice the artichokes and put into a bowl with the onion and butter. Cover with cling-film or a lid and microwave on high for 4 minutes.

Scald, skin and chop the tomatoes and add to the artichokes. Pour in the stock. Add the bouquet garni and season. Microwave on high, uncovered, for 20 minutes.

Discard the bouquet garni. Work the soup in a blender or food processor until smooth, or put through the fine blade of a vegetable mill.

Return the soup to the cleaned bowl and micro-wave on high for 2 minutes to heat through.

LEEK, POTATO AND BACON SOUP

350g/12 oz leeks
350g/12 oz potatoes
175g/6 oz lean bacon
750ml/1¼ pints stock
150ml/¼ pint milk
freshly ground black pepper

Thinly slice the leeks. Peel and slice the potatoes. Dice half the bacon. Put the leeks, potatoes and diced bacon into a roasting bag, seal loosely and microwave on high for 10 minutes.

Put the cooked vegetables and bacon into a basin and pour in the stock and milk. Season with the pepper. Microwave on high for 10 minutes.

Liquidize the soup in a blender or food processor or put through a vegetable mill.

Put the remaining bacon onto a roasting rack or onto a plate between 2 pieces of kitchen paper. Microwave on high for 2 minutes. Dice the bacon.

Return the soup to the cleaned bowl and micro-wave on high for 2–3 minutes to reheat. Serve with the diced bacon scattered on top.

CAULIFLOWER AND ALMOND SOUP

1 small cauliflower
1 medium onion, thinly sliced
1 bayleaf
100g/4 oz almonds
600ml/1 pint stock
25g/1 oz butter
2 tbsp flour
600ml/1 pint milk

Cut the cauliflower into small florets and put into a roasting bag with the onion and bayleaf. Seal loosely and microwave on high for 8 minutes.

Put the almonds into a small bowl and cover with water. Microwave on high for 3 minutes. Drain the almonds and squeeze from their skins.

Put the contents of the roasting bag, three-quarters of the almonds and the stock into a bowl. Microwave on high for 3 minutes. Discard the bayleaf and work the rest in a blender until smooth.

Put the butter into the bowl and microwave on high for 1 minute to melt. Stir in the flour and milk and microwave on high for 4 minutes, stirring at 2 minutes and again at 3 minutes. Stir in the blended cauliflower and microwave on high for 2 minutes to heat through.

Split the remaining almonds and toast until brown. Scatter over the top of the soup when serving.

SPICED AUBERGINE SLICES

450g/1 lb aubergines
2 tbsp salt
50g/2 oz almonds
6 tbsp oil
2 tbsp tomato purée
½ tsp ground cinnamon
½ tsp ground paprika
1 garlic clove, crushed with a pinch of salt

Cut the aubergines into 1-cm/½-in thick slices. Put the aubergine slices into a colander, sprinkle with salt and leave for 30 minutes to drain. Rinse through with cold water and pat dry with kitchen paper. Place on a large, flat plate.

Put the almonds into a bowl, cover with water and microwave on high for 3 minutes. Drain the almonds and squeeze from their skins.

Beat together the remaining ingredients and brush the mixture over both sides of the aubergine slices. Top each slice with 2 almonds. Microwave on high for 10 minutes. Serve hot.

HOT CHEESY AVOCADOS

2 ripe avocados
50g/2 oz salami, thinly sliced
75g/3 oz grated Cheddar cheese

Halve and stone the avocados and put into a dish. Finely chop the salami.

Fill the avocados with the salami and scatter the cheese over the top.

Cover the avocados with cling-film or a lid and microwave on high for 2 minutes. Serve hot.

STUFFED MUSHROOMS

4 large, flat mushrooms
2 tsp Dijon mustard
50g/2 oz lean cooked ham
1 small onion, finely chopped
1 garlic clove, finely chopped
25g/1 oz butter
100g/4 oz wholewheat breadcrumbs
2 tbsp chopped parsley
2 sage leaves, chopped
4 tbsp dry cider
4 small parsley sprigs

Trim and finely chop the mushroom stalks. Thinly spread each mushroom with mustard. Finely chop the ham.

Put the onion, garlic and butter into a bowl. Cover with cling-film or a lid and microwave on high for 4 minutes. Mix in the breadcrumbs, parsley, ham, mushroom stalks, sage and cider. Pile the mixture on top of the mushrooms.

Put the mushrooms on a plate and microwave on high, uncovered, for 6 minutes. Serve each one topped with a parsley sprig.

EGGS BAKED WITH MUSTARD

50g/2 oz grated Cheddar cheese
4 eggs
150ml/¼ pint double cream
2 tsp Dijon mustard
2 tbsp chopped chives

Divide the cheese between 4 individual soufflé dishes. Make a slight dent in the centre of each portion and break in an egg. Pierce the yolks with a cocktail stick.

Beat together the remaining ingredients and spoon the mixture over the eggs.

Put the soufflé dishes into the microwave and cook on high for 4 minutes. Leave to stand for 1 minute before serving.

DEVILLED PRAWNS

225g/8 oz shelled prawns
juice of ½ lemon
3 tbsp oil
1 tbsp tomato purée
1 tsp paprika
¼ tsp cayenne pepper

Divide the prawns between 4 small dishes. Beat the remaining ingredients together and spoon the mixture over the prawns.

Put the dishes into the microwave and cook on high for 2 minutes.

SMOKED MACKEREL WITH HORSERADISH CREAM

225g/8 oz smoked mackerel fillets
175g/6 oz tomatoes
150ml/¼ pint soured cream
1 tbsp grated horseradish
¼ tsp mustard powder
4 small parsley sprigs

Skin, bone and flake the mackerel. Scald, skin and finely chop the tomatoes. Mix together the soured cream, horseradish and mustard powder.

Divide the tomatoes between 4 small dishes, adding the flaked mackerel on top of each portion. Spoon the horseradish mixture over the mackerel.

Put the dishes into the microwave and cook on high for 4 minutes. Top each dish with a parsley sprig and serve hot.

CHICKEN LIVER KEBABS

225g/8 oz chicken livers
2 tbsp oil
2 tbsp dry red wine
1 tsp dried mixed herbs
1 garlic clove, crushed with a pinch of salt
freshly ground black pepper
1 green pepper

Cut the chicken livers into 2.5cm/1in pieces and put into a bowl. Beat together the oil, wine, herbs, garlic and pepper. Pour the mixture over the livers. Stir to coat the livers and leave to marinate for 1 hour at room temperature. Cut the pepper into 24 small squares.

Onto each of 8 cocktail sticks put a piece of pepper, liver, pepper, liver and pepper again. Lay the kebabs on a plate and microwave on high for 5 minutes.

FISH

Fish cooks beautifully in a microwave, staying moist, flaky and full of flavour. Fillets and fish steaks should be brushed with oil or butter and lemon juice before cooking. Whole fish should be slit or pierced in several places to prevent them from bursting. For the best results, cover the fish before cooking.

GINGERED COD WITH LIME

900g/2 lb cod fillet
15g/½ oz fresh ginger root
grated rind and juice of 1 lime
3 tbsp oil
1 tsp ground turmeric
½ tsp ground coriander
¼ tsp cayenne pepper

Skin the cod and cut into serving pieces. Put the fish into a shallow dish. Peel and grate the ginger root and mix with the remaining ingredients. Spoon the mixture over the cod. Leave the cod for 2 hours at room temperature.

Cover and microwave on high for 8 minutes. Leave to stand for 4 minutes before serving.

COD IN BEER

675g/1½ lb cod fillet
juice of 1 lemon
salt and freshly ground black pepper
150ml/¼ pint bitter beer
25g/1 oz butter
1 large onion, thinly sliced
2 tbsp wholewheat flour
4 tbsp chopped parsley

Skin the cod and cut into even-sized pieces. Put the pieces into a shallow dish, sprinkle with the lemon juice and season. Leave for 1 hour at room temperature.

Pour the beer over the cod and microwave on high for 6 minutes. Put the butter and onion into a bowl. Cover with cling-film or a lid and microwave on high for 3 minutes. Stir in the flour and the liquid from the cod. Microwave on high, uncovered, for 4 minutes, stirring after 2 minutes and again at 3 minutes. Stir in the parsley.

Pour the sauce over the fish and microwave on high for 1 minute. Leave to stand for 4 minutes before serving.

PLAICE TOPPED WITH CHEESE AND YOGHURT

4 large plaice fillets
juice of 1 lemon
freshly ground black pepper
200g/7 oz grated Cheddar cheese
125ml/4 fl oz natural yoghurt
3 tbsp chopped parsley

Put the plaice fillets, skin-side down, into a large, shallow dish. If they are too large to fit in the dish, cook them in pairs. Pour over the lemon juice and season with the pepper. Leave at room temperature for 30 minutes.

Mix together the cheese, yoghurt and parsley and spread the mixture over the plaice. Cover with cling-film or a lid and microwave on high for 6 minutes.

PLAICE WITH ANCHOVIES

8 plaice fillets
8 anchovy fillets
2 tbsp tomato purée
juice of 1 lemon

Finely chop the anchovy fillets and pound them to a paste. Mix in the tomato purée and lemon juice.

Lay 4 of the plaice fillets in a shallow dish, overlapping as little as possible. Spoon over half of the anchovy mixture. Cover and microwave on high for 4 minutes. Cook the remaining fillets in the same way.

FRESH HADDOCK WITH PRAWNS

675g/1½ lb fresh haddock fillets
juice of 1 lemon
freshly ground black pepper
4 tbsp chopped parsley
100g/4 oz shelled prawns
150ml/¼ pint double cream

Skin the fish and cut into even-sized pieces. Put the fillets into a shallow dish. Sprinkle with lemon juice and season. Leave the fish for 1 hour at room temperature.

Scatter the parsley and the prawns over the fish and spoon over the cream.

Cover and microwave on high for 6 minutes. Leave to stand for 5 minutes before serving.

SMOKED HADDOCK WITH SOURED CREAM SAUCE

675g/1½ lb smoked haddock fillets
150ml/¼ pint soured cream
grated rind of 1 lemon
3 tbsp chopped parsley
pinch of ground mace
freshly ground black pepper

Skin the fish and cut into even-sized serving pieces. Lay the pieces in a shallow dish. Mix the remaining ingredients together and spoon the mixture over the fish.

Cover the dish with a lid or cling-film and microwave on high for 5 minutes. Leave to stand for 2 minutes before serving.

SALMON WITH TARRAGON

4 salmon steaks
2 tbsp tarragon vinegar
freshly ground black pepper
1 tbsp chopped tarragon
2 tbsp chopped parsley
25g/1 oz butter

Skin the salmon steaks. Put the steaks into a shallow dish, sprinkle with tarragon vinegar and season. Leave for 1 hour at room temperature.

Scatter the tarragon and parsley over the steaks and put a knob of butter on each one. Cover and microwave on high for 6 minutes. Leave to stand for 5 minutes before serving.

TROUT COATED IN HAZELNUTS

two 450g/1 lb trout
juice of 1 lemon
75g/3 oz hazelnuts
4 tbsp chopped parsley
1 lemon, cut into wedges

Fillet the trout. Lay the fillets in a shallow dish and pour over the lemon juice. Spread the hazelnuts out on a flat plate and microwave on high for 1½ minutes. Cool the hazelnuts and grind in a liquidizer, food processor or coffee grinder. Mix with the parsley.

Microwave the fillets on high for 3 minutes. Scatter the hazelnuts on top and microwave on high for a further 2 minutes. Serve garnished with lemon wedges.

ORANGE AND LEMON TROUT

two 450g/1 lb trout
juice of 1 lemon
¼ tsp ground mace
freshly ground black pepper
2 large oranges
parsley sprigs

Fillet the trout and lay the fillets in a large, shallow dish. Pour over the lemon juice, sprinkle with mace and pepper and leave for 30 minutes at room temperature. Cut the rind and pith from the oranges. Halve each orange lengthways and cut the halves into 4 slices.

Microwave the fillets on high for 3 minutes. Lay the pieces of orange on top and microwave on high for a further 2 minutes. Serve garnished with parsley sprigs.

MACKEREL WITH MUSHROOMS

4 medium mackerel
150g/5 oz open mushrooms
1 large onion, finely chopped
1 garlic clove, finely chopped
4 tbsp oil
4 tbsp chopped parsley
3 tbsp white wine vinegar
freshly ground black pepper

Fillet the mackerel and lay the fillets in a large, shallow dish. Finely chop the mushrooms. Put into a bowl with the onion, garlic and oil. Cover with cling-film or a lid and microwave on high for 5 minutes.

Mix in the parsley and vinegar and season. Spoon the mixture over the mackerel. Cover again and microwave on high for 6 minutes.

HERRINGS IN OATMEAL

4 herrings
juice of 1 lemon
freshly ground black pepper
2 tbsp chopped thyme
50g/2 oz medium oatmeal
1 lemon, cut into wedges

Clean the herrings. Cut off the heads and slit down the belly. Open the herrings out flat, cut-side down and press down hard along the centre back. Pull out the backbones. Sprinkle the cut sides with lemon juice, pepper and thyme. Fold the fish over, reshape and coat in the oatmeal.

Lay the herrings in a shallow dish and microwave on high, uncovered, for 3 minutes. Turn the fish over and microwave on high for 3 minutes more. Leave to stand for 5 minutes. Serve garnished with lemon wedges.

HERRING AND WATERCRESS PÂTÉ

4 medium herrings, plus roes if available
1 small onion, finely chopped
50g/2 oz butter
1 tsp mustard powder
75g/3 oz watercress, finely chopped
juice of ½ lemon

Fillet the herrings. Dice the fillets and the roes (if available). Put the onion into a dish with half the butter. Cover with cling-film or a lid and microwave on high for 4 minutes. Stir in the diced herring and the mustard powder. Cover and microwave on high for 3 minutes. Add the watercress and remaining butter and microwave for 1 minute.

Put the contents of the dish into a blender or food processor. Add the lemon juice and work until smooth.

Press the mixture into an oiled 450g/1 lb loaf tin and chill for 2 hours or until firm. Cool and serve with a salad.

MEAT, POULTRY AND GAME

All cuts of meat from small chops to large joints can be successfully cooked in a microwave oven. You will find that it stays moister than when cooked in a conventional oven and large cuts hold their shape better and retain more of their original weight.

The smaller cuts do not have time to brown because their cooking time is so short. They are best covered with a sauce after or during cooking or finished under a high grill. You can also use a special browning dish or browning element if these are fitted to your microwave.

Meat casseroles are best cooked for longer periods on a simmer setting. You will also find that you need less liquid with these type of dishes. The best joints of meat for roasting are those that are boned and evenly rolled. Thinner ends should be wrapped in small pieces of aluminium foil.

Joints of meat and poultry are best cooked either covered or in a roasting bag to seal in the flavour and to help browning. The best dishes for meat are those that have a rack on which to stand the meat and a domed lid. Roasting bags should be pierced to allow steam to escape and the ends should be loosely tied with string or plastic. Never use metal tags. Cook the meat for the time required per 450g/1 lb and turn it halfway through.

When cooking is complete, the food should be allowed to stand for 15–30 minutes. If it has been cooked in a roasting bag, take it out and wrap it in aluminium foil. Food cooked in a lidded container can simply be left covered.

To help joints to brown, you can sprinkle them with herbs and spices, or baste them frequently with a marinade or sauce. Never sprinkle the meat with salt as the salt will absorb moisture and cause the meat to toughen.

A meat thermometer is a useful method of testing whether the meat is done, but never put the thermometer into the cooker unless it has been specially designed for microwave use.

When cooking large poultry such as a turkey, you may find that small areas of the bird are over-cooking. This will be indicated by the appearance of a large golden brown spot. Should this occur, anchor small pieces of foil over these areas with cocktail sticks.

Always thaw frozen meat before cooking. Put the meat into the oven on the defrost setting for the required amount of time, wrap it in foil and allow it to stand so the heat can gradually spread through evenly.

PORK BURGERS

900g/2 lb belly pork rashers
1 small onion
½ tsp salt
1 tsp black peppercorns, coarsely crushed
1 tsp dried sage
50g/2 oz wholewheat flour
quick apple sauce for serving (p. 72)

Cut the rinds and any bones from the pork. Finely mince the meat with the onion. Mix in the salt, peppercorns and sage. Form the mixture into 8 round, flat burger shapes and coat in flour. Put the burger shapes on a large, flat dish and leave in the refrigerator for 30 minutes to set into shape.

Put the burgers on a rack in a dish and microwave on high for 15 minutes. Leave for 10 minutes before serving. Serve the hot apple sauce separately.

PORK CHOPS WITH MUSTARD

4 pork chops
2 tbsp mustard powder
2 tbsp dry white wine
1 tsp honey
4 sage leaves, chopped

Cut the rind from the chops. Mix together the mustard powder, wine, honey and sage leaves.

Spread the mixture over one side of the chops.

Put the chops on a rack over a flat dish. Microwave on high for 12 minutes. Leave for 5 minutes before serving.

SWEET AND SOUR ROAST PORK

1.8kg/4 lb pork shoulder, in one piece
4 tbsp soy sauce
2 tbsp tomato purée
2 tbsp cider vinegar
1 tbsp honey

Cut the rind from the pork. Weigh the meat and put on a rack in a roasting dish, fat-side down. Mix together the remaining ingredients. Spoon half the barbeque mixture over the pork and cover the dish.

Calculate the cooking time at 9 minutes per 450g/1 lb. Microwave on high for half that amount of time. Turn the pork over and spoon over half the remaining barbeque mixture. Cover it again and microwave on high for half the remaining time. Spoon over the remaining mixture. Cover and complete the cooking time. Leave the pork standing, covered, for 15 minutes before carving.

HAM IN RED WINE SAUCE

**450g/1 lb lean, cooked, unpressed ham, cut
into 6-mm/¼-in thick slices**
1 large onion, quartered and thinly sliced
25g/1 oz butter
3 tbsp flour
450ml/¾ pint dry red wine

Cut the ham into even-sized pieces about
5 × 2.5cm/2 × 1in. Put the onion and butter into a
dish. Cover with cling-film or a lid and microwave
on high for 4 minutes. Stir in the flour and wine.
Microwave on high, uncovered, for 4 minutes
more.

Put in the pieces of ham. Microwave on high for
2 minutes to heat it through.

MINCED BEEF WITH TOMATOES

675g/1½ lb minced beef
450g/1 lb tomatoes
2 medium onions, thinly sliced
1 garlic clove, finely chopped
1 tbsp chopped thyme
2 tbsp chopped parsley
¼ tsp Tabasco sauce

Put the minced beef into a bowl. Scald, skin and
chop the tomatoes and add to the beef. Mix in the
remaining ingredients.

Cover with cling-film or a lid and microwave on
high for 15 minutes, stopping after 5 minutes and
again after 10 minutes to break up the meat. Leave
the beef to stand for 5 minutes before serving.

BEEF WITH RATATOUILLE

450g/1 lb braising steak
350g/12 oz courgettes
1 red pepper
1 green pepper
350g/12 oz aubergines
100g/4 oz mushrooms
1 large onion, thinly sliced
1 garlic clove, finely chopped
25g/1 oz butter
125ml/4 fl oz dry red wine
1 tbsp tomato purée
bouquet garni
salt and freshly ground black pepper

Cut the beef into 2.5cm/1 in cubes. Thinly slice the courgettes. Cut the peppers into 2.5cm/1 in strips. Dice the aubergines and thinly slice the mushrooms.

Put the onion and garlic into a casserole with the butter. Cover with cling-film or a lid and microwave on high for 4 minutes. Add the beef and microwave on high, uncovered, for 3 minutes. Mix in the vegetables.

Mix together the wine and tomato purée and pour into the casserole. Put in the bouquet garni and season. Cover and microwave on a simmer setting for 55 minutes. Remove the bouquet garni. Leave the casserole to stand for 15 minutes before serving.

ROAST SIRLOIN OF BEEF

1.575–1.8kg/3½–4 lb sirloin beef
6 tbsp Worcestershire sauce
6 tbsp mushroom ketchup

Check the weight of the beef. Mix the sauce and ketchup together. Put the beef on a rack in a roasting dish. Brush with the sauce mixture. Cover with a lid or put into a roasting bag.

Microwave on high for 5½ minutes per 450g/1 lb for rare, 7½ minutes per 450g/1 lb for medium or 9 minutes per 450g/1 lb for well done. Turn the meat over halfway through and brush with more sauce mixture every 3 minutes.

After cooking, leave the beef covered for 15 minutes before slicing. Serves 6–8.

VEAL ESCALOPES WITH MUSHROOMS

4 veal escalopes
1 small onion, finely chopped
25g/1 oz butter
100g/4 oz button mushrooms, thinly sliced
¼ tsp dill seeds
grated rind and juice of ½ lemon
5 tbsp soured cream
5 tbsp stock
2 tsp paprika
parsley sprigs

Beat the escalopes out flat and cut each one in half lengthways. Put the onion and butter into a dish. Cover and microwave on high for 3 minutes. Add the escalopes and coat with the butter. Cover and microwave on high for 3 minutes.

Add the mushrooms and sprinkle in the dill seeds and lemon rind. Mix together the lemon juice, soured cream, stock and paprika. Pour the sauce over the veal. Cover and microwave on high for 15 minutes, leave the veal to stand for 10 minutes. Serve garnished with parsley sprigs.

TANDOORI LAMB

1 leg of lamb
300ml/½ pint natural yoghurt
grated rind and juice of 1 lemon
25g/1 oz fresh ginger root, peeled and grated
2 tsp cumin seeds
2 tsp ground coriander
¼ tsp chilli powder

Check the weight of the lamb and put in a non-metal dish. Mix together the remaining ingredients and spoon over the lamb, making sure it is well coated. Cover and leave for 48 hours in a cool place.

Put the lamb on a rack in a roasting dish and baste with the marinade. Cover the thin end with aluminium foil. Put on a lid or put the dish into a roasting bag.

Microwave on high for 8 minutes per 450g/1 lb, turning the lamb over halfway through and removing the foil for the final 15 minutes. Leave the lamb covered for 15 minutes before carving. Serves 6–8.

LAMB CHOPS TOPPED WITH BLUE CHEESE

4 large lamb chops
salt and pepper
100g/4 oz grated blue cheese
1 small onion, very finely chopped
4 tbsp chopped parsley

Trim the chops of any excess fat, season and lay on a rack in a roasting dish. Cover and microwave on high for 5 minutes. Turn the chops over, cover again and microwave on high for a further 5 minutes.

Mix together the cheese, onion and parsley. Press the mixture on top of the chops. Cover again and microwave on high for 2 minutes.

LIVER, BACON AND MUSHROOMS

575g/1¼ lb lambs' liver
25g/1 oz wholewheat flour
100g/4 oz streaky bacon
1 large onion, thinly sliced
15g/½ oz butter
225g/8 oz open mushrooms, thinly sliced
2 tbsp chopped thyme
300ml/½ pint stock
2 tbsp tomato purée
freshly ground black pepper

Cut the liver into thin slices and coat in the flour. Finely chop the bacon.

Put the bacon, onion and butter into a dish and cover with cling-film or a lid. Microwave on high for 4 minutes. Mix in the liver, mushrooms and thyme. Beat the stock and tomato purée together and pour over the liver. Season with the pepper.

Cover and microwave on high for 5 minutes. Turn the liver, cover again and microwave on high for a further 5 minutes. Leave to stand for 5 minutes before serving.

CURRIED ROAST CHICKEN

one 1.575-kg/3½-lb roasting chicken
300ml/½ pint soured cream
4 tsp curry powder
2 tbsp mango chutney
1 garlic clove, crushed with a pinch of salt

Put the chicken, breast down on a rack in a cooking tray. Beat the soured cream with the curry powder, chutney and garlic. Spoon half of the mixture over the chicken.

Either put the chicken into a roasting bag or cover the tray with a lid. Microwave on high for 15 minutes. Turn the chicken breast-side up and spoon over the remaining soured cream mixture, making sure that every part of the chicken skin is coated.

Microwave on high for a further 15 minutes. Leave the chicken to stand for 15 minutes before carving.

CHICKEN IN SHERRY

one 1.575-kg/3½-lb roasting chicken
100g/4 oz smoked streaky bacon
225g/8 oz tomatoes
1 medium onion, finely chopped
1 garlic clove, finely chopped
150ml/¼ pint dry sherry
4 tbsp chopped parsley

Joint the chicken. Finely chop the bacon. Scald, skin and chop the tomatoes.

Put the onion, garlic and bacon into a casserole. Cover with cling-film or a lid and microwave on high for 4 minutes. Add the chicken joints, place the tomatoes on top and pour in the sherry.

Cover and microwave on high for 30 minutes. Leave to stand for 15 minutes before serving. Serve in a warm dish, scattered with parsley.

ROAST PHEASANT WITH REDCURRANT GLAZE

1 pheasant
bouquet garni
3 tbsp redcurrant jelly
2 tbsp dry red wine
4 juniper berries
4 allspice berries
4 black peppercorns

Truss the pheasant, putting the bouquet garni inside. Place the pheasant breast-side down, on a rack in a dish. Cover with a lid or put into a roasting bag. Microwave on high for 10 minutes.

Using a pestle and mortar, crush together the juniper, allspice and peppercorns. Put the redcurrant jelly, wine and crushed spices into a bowl. Microwave on high for 1½ minutes for the jelly to melt.

Turn the pheasant breast-side up and baste with half of the redcurrant jelly mixture. Cover again and microwave on high for 5 minutes. Baste with the remaining redcurrant jelly and microwave on high for a further 5 minutes. Leave to stand for 15 minutes before carving.

EGGS AND CHEESE

Eggs and cheese take an extremely short time to cook in a microwave oven and so can make quick and easy main meals and snacks.

Ideally, eggs should be at room temperature before cooking. They should never be cooked in their shells and, when cooking them whole, it is a good idea to pierce the yolks with a cocktail stick or fine skewer to prevent them from bursting.

Soufflés cannot be made in a microwave oven but you can produce very successful soufflé omelettes and thick filled omelettes. Scrambled eggs can be prepared quickly and easily.

Always remember that eggs will continue to cook for a time after they are removed from the microwave oven so it is better to slightly under-cook them. Many main dishes based on cheese can be made in the microwave oven and cheese can also be slowly melted to be spooned over toast.

EGGS BAKED WITH TUNA AND TOMATOES

one 200-g/7-oz tin tuna fish
450g/1 lb tomatoes
1 medium onion, finely chopped
1 garlic clove, finely chopped
3 tbsp oil
pinch of cayenne pepper
2 tbsp chopped parsley
4 eggs

Drain and flake the tuna. Scald, skin and finely chop the tomatoes. Put the onion, garlic and oil into a shallow dish. Cover with cling-film or a lid and microwave on high for 4 minutes.

Mix in the tuna, tomatoes, pepper and parsley. Make 4 indentations in the mixture using the back of a tablespoon and break an egg into each one. Cover and microwave on high for 6 minutes. Leave the eggs for 2 minutes before serving.

EGGS BAKED WITH CHEESE AND CREAM

4 large eggs
butter for greasing
150g/5 oz grated Cheddar cheese
150ml/¼ pint double cream
½ tsp curry powder
½ tsp paprika

Break the eggs into a greased, flat, ovenproof dish and pierce each yolk with a skewer or cocktail stick. Scatter the cheese over the eggs. Mix the cream with the curry powder and paprika and spoon the mixture over the top. Microwave the eggs for 5 minutes, checking at 2 minutes and 4 minutes. Serve straight from the dish.

HAM AND CHEESE SCRAMBLE

6 eggs
4 tbsp milk
175g/6 oz lean cooked ham
75g/3 oz grated Cheddar cheese
freshly ground black pepper
25g/1 oz butter
8 slices wholewheat toast, buttered

In a large bowl, beat the eggs with the milk. Finely dice the ham. Mix the ham and cheese into the eggs and season with the pepper. Cut the butter into small pieces and put on top of the scramble.

Microwave on high, uncovered, for 6 minutes, stirring with a fork and turning after each 2 minutes. Stir again and leave the scramble to stand for 2 minutes before serving, piled onto the toast.

SALAMI AND TOMATO SCRAMBLE

100g/4 oz salami, thinly sliced
225g/8 oz tomatoes
1 medium onion, finely chopped
25g/1 oz butter
6 eggs, beaten

Chop the salami. Scald, skin and chop the tomatoes. Put the onion into a bowl with the butter. Cover with cling-film or a lid and micro-wave on high for 2 minutes. Mix in the salami, cover again and microwave on high for a further 2 minutes.

Stir in the eggs and tomatoes. Microwave on high, uncovered, for 3 minutes, stirring after 1 minute and again after 2 minutes. Stir and leave the scramble for 1 minute before serving.

Either pile the scramble onto hot buttered toast or serve accompanied by jacket potatoes.

MUSHROOM AND AVOCADO OMELETTE

225g/8 oz button mushrooms
1 large onion, thinly sliced
25g/1 oz butter
1 ripe avocado
6 eggs
4 tbsp chopped parsley
salt and pepper

Thinly slice the mushrooms and put into a shallow 25cm/10in dish with the onion and butter. Cover with cling-film and microwave on high for 5 minutes.

Peel, stone and mash the avocado. Beat in the eggs, one at a time so you have a smooth mixture. Mix in the parsley and season. Pour the mixture over the mushrooms, making sure that it is evenly distributed. Microwave on high for 8 minutes, checking and turning every 2 minutes.

PEPPER OMELETTE

1 red pepper
1 green pepper
1 large onion, quartered and thinly sliced
1 garlic clove, finely crushed
25g/1 oz butter
6 eggs
100g/4 oz grated Cheddar cheese
salt and freshly ground black pepper

Core and seed the peppers and cut into 2.5cm/1in strips. Put the strips into a round 2.5-cm/1-in deep, 20-cm/8-in diameter dish with the onion and garlic. Dot with the butter and cover with cling-film. Microwave on high for 6 minutes.

Beat the eggs with the cheese and seasonings. Pour into the dish, distributing the mixture evenly. Microwave on high for 8 minutes, checking and turning every 2 minutes. Cut the omelette into quarters and serve straight from the dish.

KIPPER SOUFFLÉ OMELETTE

175g/6 oz kipper fillets
6 eggs, separated
1 tbsp tomato purée
2 tbsp chopped parsley
225g/8 oz tomatoes, sliced into rings

Put the kipper fillets into a bowl, cover with water and microwave on high for 6 minutes. Lift out the fillets. Skin, bone and flake them.

Beat the egg yolks with the tomato purée. Mix in the flaked kippers and the parsley. Stiffly whip the egg whites and fold into the yolks. Put the mixture into a shallow 25cm/10in dish.

Microwave on high for 4 minutes. Lay the tomato rings on top and microwave on high for a further 1 minute. Leave the omelette to stand for 2 minutes before serving.

CHEESE, LEEK AND POTATO PIE

675g/1½ lb small potatoes
450g/1 lb leeks
25g/1 oz butter
2 tbsp flour
300ml/½ pint milk
2 tsp spiced granular mustard
225g/8 oz grated Cheshire cheese
4 tbsp chopped parsley
4 sage leaves, chopped

Scrub and prick the potatoes. Microwave on high for 10 minutes, turning them over halfway through. Thinly slice.

Thinly slice the leeks and put into a bowl with the butter. Cover with cling-film or a lid and microwave on high for 10 minutes. Stir in the flour, milk and mustard. Microwave on high, uncovered, for 4 minutes, stirring after the first 2 minutes. Beat in 175g/6 oz of the cheese, together with the parsley and sage.

Layer the potatoes and leek mixture in a deep dish or pie dish, finishing with potatoes. Cover with the remaining cheese. Microwave on high, uncovered, for 2 minutes for the cheese to melt.

CHEESE AND TOMATO RISOTTO

1 large red pepper
1 large onion, finely chopped
25g/1 oz butter
225g/8 oz short grain brown rice
1 tbsp tomato purée
600ml/1 pint chicken stock, boiling
1 tsp paprika
salt and freshly ground black pepper
225g/8 oz Gruyère cheese
450g/1 lb tomatoes
2 tbsp chopped parsley

Core, seed and finely chop the pepper. Put into a bowl with the onion and butter. Cover with cling-film or a lid and microwave on high for 4 minutes.

Stir in the rice, tomato purée, stock, paprika and seasonings. Microwave on high, covered, for 20 minutes. Take out and allow to stand for 15 minutes.

Finely grate the cheese and chop the tomatoes. Mix first the cheese and then the tomatoes into the risotto. Serve scattered with chopped parsley.

TAGLIATELLE WITH COURGETTES AND CHEESE

225g/8 oz wholewheat tagliatelle
5 tbsp oil
1 tsp salt
350g/12 oz courgettes
50g/2 oz shelled walnuts
1 large onion, thinly sliced
1 garlic clove, finely chopped
25g/1 oz butter
1 tbsp tomato purée
2 tbsp flour
300ml/½ pint milk
150g/5 oz grated Cheddar cheese

Pour boiling water into a large bowl. Put in 1 tbsp oil, add the tagliatelle and season. Cover with cling-film or a lid and microwave on high for 12 minutes. Leave the tagliatelle for 10 minutes before draining.

While the tagliatelle is cooking, finely chop the courgettes and grind the walnuts. Put the courgettes, onion and garlic into a bowl with the remaining oil. Cover with cling-film or a lid and microwave on high for 10 minutes. Mix the courgettes and ground walnuts into the drained pasta and put into an ovenproof dish.

Put the butter into a bowl and microwave on high for 30 seconds to melt. Stir in the tomato purée, flour and milk. Microwave on high for 4 minutes, stirring after the first 2 minutes. Beat in three-quarters of the cheese and pour the sauce over the tagliatelle. Scatter the remaining cheese over the top. Microwave on high for 2 minutes.

CHEESE RAMEKINS

2 large slices bread, toasted
approximately 1 tbsp anchovy paste
butter for greasing
2 eggs
50g/2 oz grated Cheddar cheese
300ml/½ pint milk
freshly ground black pepper

Spread the toast with the anchovy paste and cut into small cubes. Divide between 4 buttered ramekin dishes.

Beat the eggs together, stir in the cheese and milk and season well. Pour the mixture over the anchovy toast.

Put the ramekins into the microwave and cook on low for 12 minutes.

CHEESE FONDUE

300ml/½ pint dry white wine
1 garlic clove, crushed with a pinch of salt
225g/8 oz grated Gruyère cheese
225g/8 oz grated Cheddar cheese
25g/1 oz cornflour
freshly ground black pepper
2 tbsp brandy
wholewheat bread, toasted and cut into cubes

Put the wine and garlic into a bowl. Cover and microwave on low for 8 minutes. Mix the cheeses with the cornflour and gradually beat the mixture into the wine. Season well. Microwave on low for 6 minutes, stirring every minute so the cheese melts. Stir in the brandy. Microwave on low for 1 minute.

The fondue can be served straight from the dish and reheated when necessary, or it can be transferred to a fondue burner. On serving, each person dips cubes of toast into the cheese.

VEGETABLES

Vegetables can be cooked quickly and healthily in a microwave oven with very little liquid and without fat. They retain a good natural colour and a crisp but tender texture.

Vegetables can be cooked in covered containers or sealed in roasting bags. Pierce the skin of whole vegetables such as potatoes or tomatoes to prevent bursting and arrange them round the edge of a dish. If you have vegetables of uneven shapes, such as broccoli, arrange them with the thinner ends pointing inwards. Finely chopped vegetables or small loose vegetables such as garden peas are best when spread evenly in a shallow container.

Never salt vegetables before cooking as this can cause them to dry and toughen.

RUNNER BEANS AND BACON

675g/1½ lb runner beans
75g/3 oz bacon
1 large onion, thinly sliced
25g/1 oz butter
2 tbsp chopped thyme
2 tbsp water

String and slice the beans. Finely chop the bacon. Put the bacon, onion and butter into a dish and microwave on high for 2 minutes. Mix in the beans and thyme and add the water. Cover with cling-film or a lid and microwave on high for 15 minutes.

CAULIFLOWER, PEPPER AND TOMATOES

1 medium cauliflower
1 green pepper
350g/12 oz tomatoes
1 tbsp grated Parmesan cheese

Cut the cauliflower into florets and put into a shallow dish. Core and seed the pepper and cut into strips. Scald, skin and chop the tomatoes. Scatter over the cauliflower.

Cover with cling-film or a lid and microwave on high for 20 minutes. Scatter the Parmesan cheese over the top just before serving.

CHICORY WITH ORANGE

675g/1½ lb chicory (Belgian endive)
juice of 1 large orange
4 tbsp chopped parsley

Cut the chicory into 2-cm/¾-in thick diagonal slices and put into a bowl. Pour in the orange juice and mix in the parsley. Cover with cling-film or a lid and microwave on high for 10 minutes.

BRAISED CELERY

1 head of celery
1 large onion, quartered and thinly sliced
1 large carrot, finely chopped
2 sage leaves, chopped
6 tbsp stock
25g/1 oz butter
salt and freshly ground pepper

Cut the celery sticks into 7.5cm/3in lengths. Put into a bowl with the onion, carrot, sage and stock. Dot with butter and season. Cover with cling-film or a lid. Microwave on high for 12 minutes.

HOT COURGETTE SALAD

675g/1½ lb courgettes
4 tbsp oil
1 tbsp white vinegar
1 tbsp tomato purée
½ tsp Tabasco sauce
1 tsp paprika
1 garlic clove, crushed with a pinch of salt

Thinly slice the courgettes and put into a round, high-sided dish. Beat the remaining ingredients together and spoon over the courgettes.

Cover the dish with cling-film, making 2 slits in the top. Microwave the courgettes for 12 minutes. Remove and allow to stand for 2 minutes before serving.

AUBERGINES IN WHITE WINE

450g/1 lb aubergines
2 tbsp salt
100g/4 oz mushrooms
6 tbsp dry white wine
1 tbsp tomato purée
1 medium onion, thinly sliced
1 garlic clove, finely chopped
3 tbsp oil
1 tbsp chopped thyme

Cut the aubergines in half lengthways. Cut the halves into 1-cm/½-in thick slices. Put the aubergine slices into a colander and sprinkle with salt. Leave for 30 minutes to drain. Rinse through with cold water and dry with kitchen paper. Thinly slice the mushrooms. Mix together the wine and tomato purée.

Put the onion, garlic and oil into a casserole. Cover with cling-film or a lid and microwave on high for 4 minutes. Mix in the aubergines and mushrooms, thyme and wine mixture. Cover again and microwave on high for 15 minutes.

CARROTS WITH PAPRIKA

500g/1 lb 2 oz carrots
1 tsp paprika
1 tbsp tomato purée
4 tbsp water
15g/½ oz butter

Thinly slice the carrots and put into a dish. Mix the paprika and tomato purée with the water and pour over the carrots. Dot with butter. Cover and microwave on high for 15 minutes.

LEEKS WITH MUSTARD

450g/1 lb leeks
4 tbsp chopped parsley
1 tsp Dijon mustard
4 tbsp stock
25g/1 oz butter

Wash the leeks well. Cut the leeks in half length-ways and then into 1cm/½in slices. Put into a bowl and add the parsley.

Mix the Dijon mustard into the stock and pour the mixture over the leeks. Dot with the butter. Cover with cling-film or a lid and microwave on high for 8 minutes.

SPICED BUTTERED CABBAGE

1 large green cabbage
8 juniper berries
4 allspice berries
4 black peppercorns
pinch of salt
1 garlic clove, finely chopped
25g/1 oz butter, cut into small pieces

Shred the cabbage. Using a pestle and mortar, crush together the juniper, allspice, peppercorns, salt and garlic.

Put one-third of the cabbage into a large dish. Sprinkle in half the spice mixture and dot with half the butter. Put in another one-third of the cabbage, the remaining spice mixture and the remaining cabbage. Dot with the remaining butter.

Cover the dish and microwave on high for 10 minutes.

BRAISED RED CABBAGE

675g/1½ lb red cabbage
1 large cooking apple
1 large onion, thinly sliced
2 tbsp redcurrant jelly
2 tbsp red wine vinegar

Shred the cabbage. Core and thinly slice the apple. Mix together in a casserole and add the onion, redcurrant jelly and vinegar. Cover and microwave on high for 10 minutes. Stir and microwave on high for a further 10 minutes.

MUSHROOMS WITH LEMON

225g/8 oz button mushrooms
25g/1 oz butter
juice of ½ lemon
4 tbsp chopped parsley

Thinly slice the mushrooms and put into a bowl with the butter, lemon juice and parsley. Cover with cling–film or a lid and microwave on high for 5 minutes.

PEAS IN CREAM

900g/2 lb peas, weighed before shelling
150ml/¼ pint double cream
1 tsp honey
3 tbsp chopped parsley

Shell the peas and put into a bowl or casserole with the cream, honey and parsley. Cover with cling-film or a lid and microwave on high for 5 minutes. Stir, cover again and microwave on high for a further 5 minutes.

★ *450g/1 lb frozen peas may be used instead of fresh peas.*

SWEETCORN WITH PEPPERS

one 350-g/12-oz tin sweetcorn
1 red pepper
1 green pepper
1 large onion, thinly sliced
15g/½ oz butter
1 tbsp chopped thyme

Drain the sweetcorn. Core and seed the peppers and cut into 2.5cm/1in strips. Put the pepper strips into a bowl with the onion and butter. Cover and microwave on high for 3 minutes. Mix in the sweetcorn and thyme, cover again and microwave on high for a further 3 minutes.

BROAD BEANS IN CIDER

900g/2 lb broad beans, weighed before shelling
150ml/¼ pint dry cider
1 tbsp chopped savory

Shell the beans and put into a casserole with the cider and savory. Cover with cling-film or a lid and microwave on high for 5 minutes. Stir, cover again and microwave on high for a further 5 minutes.
★ *350g/12 oz frozen beans may be used instead of fresh beans.*

POTATOES IN SOURED CREAM

675g/1½ lb small potatoes
1 large onion, thinly sliced
25g/1 oz butter
50g/2 oz grated Cheddar cheese
¼ nutmeg, grated
4 tbsp chopped parsley
4 sage leaves, chopped
freshly ground black pepper
200ml/7 fl oz soured cream
200ml/7 fl oz milk
1 garlic clove, crushed with a pinch of salt
2 bayleaves

Scrub and thinly slice the potatoes. Put the onion into a bowl with the butter. Cover with cling-film or a lid and microwave on high for 4 minutes. Layer the potatoes and onion in a casserole, scattering in half the cheese, the nutmeg and herbs and seasoning with pepper. Top with the remaining cheese.

Beat together the soured cream, milk and garlic and pour into the casserole. Tuck in the bayleaves. Cover and microwave on high for 30 minutes.

This is a very rich dish that is best served with plainly cooked meats.

RICE AND PASTA

White rice cooks only a fraction quicker in a micro-wave oven than in a saucepan on the hob, but cooking time for brown rice is much quicker, even allowing for the standing time. Both white and brown rice cook perfectly and never become sticky.

Pasta takes almost as long in a microwave oven as on a hob, but the sauces that so often accompany pasta can be made quickly during the standing time, so the total cooking time for the whole dish can frequently be made shorter.

WHITE RICE

225g/8 oz long grain white rice
600ml/1 pint water, boiling
1 tsp salt
1 tbsp oil

Put the rice into a bowl with the water, salt and oil. Cover and microwave on high for 10 minutes. Leave the rice to stand, covered, for 10 minutes before serving.

BROWN RICE

225g/8 oz long grain brown rice
600ml/1 pint water, boiling
1 tsp salt
1 tbsp oil

Put the rice into a bowl or casserole with the water, salt and oil. Cover and microwave on high for 20 minutes. Leave the rice to stand, covered, for 15 minutes before serving.

RICE IN STOCK

1 medium onion, finely chopped
25g/1 oz butter or 4 tbsp oil
225g/8 oz long grain white rice
600ml/1 pint stock, boiling
1 tsp salt

Put the onion into a bowl or casserole with the butter or oil. Cover with cling-film or a lid and microwave on high for 3 minutes. Stir in the rice, cover and microwave on high for 1 minute.

Pour in the stock, add the salt, cover and micro-wave on high for 10 minutes. Leave the rice to stand for 10 minutes before serving.

★ *For long grain brown rice, cook for 20 minutes after adding the stock and leave the rice for 15 minutes before serving.*

CURRY RICE WITH MUSHROOMS

1 medium onion, thinly sliced
1 garlic clove, finely chopped
25g/1 oz butter
100g/4 oz button mushrooms, thinly sliced
2 tsp curry powder
225g/8 oz long grain white rice
600ml/1 pint stock, boiling
pinch of salt

Put the onion, garlic and butter into a bowl, cover with cling-film or a lid and microwave on high for 3 minutes. Stir in the mushrooms and curry powder. Cover and microwave on high for 2 minutes. Stir in the rice, cover again and microwave on high for 1 minute.

Pour in the stock and add the salt. Microwave on high, covered, for 10 minutes. Leave the rice to stand for 10 minutes before serving.

PEANUT AND RAISIN PILAFF

1 medium onion, thinly sliced
25g/1 oz butter
1 tsp ground turmeric
225g/8 oz long grain white rice
600ml/1 pint water, boiling
pinch of salt
50g/2 oz peanuts
50g/2 oz raisins

Put the onion into a bowl with the butter and turmeric. Cover with cling-film or a lid and microwave on high for 4 minutes. Stir in the rice, cover again and microwave on high for 1 minute.

Pour in the water and add the salt. Microwave on high, covered, for 5 minutes. Mix in the peanuts and raisins and cook for 5 minutes. Leave the rice to stand for 10 minutes before serving.

PASTA

225g/8 oz pasta
boiling water
1 tbsp oil
1 tsp salt

Put the boiling water into a large bowl. Add the oil and salt and put in the pasta, bending spaghetti or lasagne to fit the bowl.

Cover with cling-film or a lid and microwave on high for 12 minutes. Leave the pasta to stand, covered, for 10 minutes before draining.
★ *Both wholewheat and white pasta can be cooked in this way.*

PASTA SHELLS IN ANCHOVY AND TOMATO SAUCE

225g/8 oz wholewheat pasta shells
boiling water
4 tbsp oil
1 tsp salt
1 medium onion, finely chopped
1 garlic clove, finely chopped
1 tbsp flour
200ml/7 fl oz tomato juice
6 anchovy fillets, chopped
1 tbsp fresh or 2 tsp dried basil

Put the pasta into a bowl with the water, 1 tbsp of the oil and the salt. Cover and microwave on high for 12 minutes. Leave the pasta to stand, covered, for 10 minutes before draining.

Make the sauce while the pasta is standing. Put the onion and garlic into a bowl with the remaining oil. Cover with cling-film or a lid and microwave on high for 4 minutes. Stir in the flour and tomato juice. Add the anchovies and basil. Microwave on high, uncovered, for 2 minutes. Stir and cook for a further 2 minutes. Coat the pasta with the sauce and serve as an accompaniment to plain cooked meat dishes.

SPAGHETTI WITH CREAM CHEESE

225g/8 oz wholewheat spaghetti
boiling water
1 tbsp oil
1 tsp salt
1 small onion, finely chopped
1 garlic clove, finely chopped
25g/1 oz butter
100g/4 oz cream cheese
1 tbsp chopped thyme
2 tbsp chopped parsley

Lower the spaghetti into a bowl containing the water and add the oil and salt. Cover and microwave on high for 12 minutes. Leave to stand for 10 minutes before draining.

Prepare the cheese while the spaghetti is standing. Put the onion and garlic into a bowl with the butter. Cover with cling-film or a lid and microwave on high for 4 minutes. Mix in the cheese and herbs. Microwave on high for 45 seconds. Fold the cheese mixture into the spaghetti.

Serve hot as an accompaniment to cold meats or to egg dishes.

⋆ *A low-fat soft cheese may be used instead of cream cheese.*

GREEN TAGLIATELLE AND OLIVE SALAD

175g/6 oz tagliatelle verdi
boiling water
6 tbsp oil
1 tsp salt
1 medium onion, thinly sliced
1 garlic clove, crushed with a pinch of salt
2 tbsp white wine vinegar
freshly ground black pepper
16 black olives
4 tbsp chopped parsley
225g/8 oz tomatoes

Put the boiling water into a large bowl. Put in the tagliatelle, 1 tsp of the oil and the salt. Cover with cling-film or a lid and microwave on high for 12 minutes. Leave the tagliatelle, covered, for 10 minutes before draining.

Put the onion and garlic into a bowl with the remaining oil. Cover with cling-film or a lid and microwave on high for 2 minutes. Add the vinegar and season with the pepper. Stir the onion dressing into the tagliatelle. Leave the tagliatelle until it is cold.

Halve and stone the olives and mix into the salad with the parsley. Put the salad onto a serving plate and garnish with the tomatoes, cut into rings or wedges.

SNACK MEALS

A microwave oven is perfect for cooking quick snacks for the family at any time of the day. Base snacks on vegetables, pasta, rice or bread or cheap meat products like sausages.

When heating bread, lay it on a double layer of kitchen paper to prevent it from becoming moist or soggy.

HOT BACON AND CHEESE SANDWICHES

8 streaky bacon rashers
8 slices wholewheat bread
butter
4 tbsp chutney
100g/4 oz grated Cheddar cheese

Put the bacon rashers onto a plate between 2 pieces of kitchen paper. Microwave on high for 4 minutes. Cut the rashers to fit the bread slices.

Butter the bread and spread 4 of the slices with chutney. Lay the bacon on top and cover with cheese. Make sandwiches using the remaining bread slices.

Cover a plate with a double layer of kitchen paper. Put the sandwiches, 2 at a time, onto the plate. Microwave each pair on high for 2 minutes.

SARDINE BAPS

three 100-g/4-oz tins sardines in oil
juice of ½ lemon
4 tbsp chopped parsley
1 small onion, very finely chopped
4 baps
butter
4 tomatoes

Drain the sardines. Mash with the lemon juice and mix in the parsley and onion.

Split and butter the baps. Spread the sardine mixture on the base of each one. Cut the tomatoes into rings and lay them on top. Put the tops on the baps.

Cover a plate with a double layer of kitchen paper. Put the baps, 2 at a time, onto the plate and microwave each pair on high for 2 minutes.

BARBEQUED BAKED BEANS AND BACON

225g/8 oz lean bacon rashers
two 450-g/1-lb tins baked beans
2 tbsp tomato purée
2 tbsp Worcestershire sauce
2 tbsp soy sauce
2 rings fresh pineapple (optional)

Put the bacon rashers onto a plate between 2 pieces of kitchen paper. Microwave on high for 4 minutes. Finely chop the bacon.

In a bowl, mix together the beans, tomato purée, Worcestershire and soy sauces and bacon. Cover with cling-film or a lid and microwave on high for 3 minutes.

If using, chop the pineapple into chunks and mix into the beans. Cover again and microwave on high for 30 seconds.

MUSHROOMS AND HAM IN CREAM

350g/12 oz button mushrooms
225g/8 oz lean cooked ham
25g/1 oz butter
150ml/¼ pint double cream
1 tsp Dijon mustard
2 tbsp chopped parsley
1 tbsp chopped thyme

Thinly slice the mushrooms and finely chop the ham. Put the mushrooms into a dish with the butter. Cover with cling-film or a lid and micro-wave on high for 4 minutes.

Mix together the cream and mustard and stir into the mushrooms, together with the ham and herbs. Cover again and microwave on high for 2 minutes.

Serve either piled onto hot buttered toast or with jacket potatoes.

SWEETCORN SAVOURY

one 350-g/12-oz tin sweetcorn
about 300ml/½ pint milk
1 large onion, thinly sliced
1 green pepper, de-seeded and cut into strips
25g/1 oz butter
3 tbsp wholewheat flour
100g/4 oz lean cooked ham, diced
75g/3 oz grated Cheddar cheese
8 slices toast, buttered

Drain the sweetcorn and reserve the liquid. Make the liquid up to 300ml/½ pint with milk. Put the onion, pepper and butter into a dish and microwave on high for 5 minutes. Stir in the flour and the milk mixture and microwave on high for 4 minutes. Stir in the ham and sweetcorn and microwave for 1 minute. Stir in the cheese and microwave for a further 30 seconds.

To serve, pile the mixture onto the buttered toast.

CORNED BEEF AND POTATO CASSEROLE

225g/8 oz corned beef, sliced
675g/1½ lb small potatoes
450g/1 lb tomatoes
1 large onion, thinly sliced
25g/1 oz butter
4 tbsp chopped parsley
4 sage leaves, chopped
1 tsp paprika
pinch of cayenne pepper

Chop the corned beef. Scrub and thinly slice the potatoes. Scald, skin and slice the tomatoes. Put the onion into a bowl with the butter. Cover with cling-film or a lid and microwave on high for 4 minutes.

In a casserole, layer the potatoes, onion, corned beef and tomatoes, scattering in the herbs, paprika and cayenne pepper between each layer. End with a layer of tomatoes. Cover with cling-film or a lid and microwave on high for 30 minutes.

SPAGHETTI WITH TUNA AND TOMATO SAUCE

225g/8 oz wholewheat spaghetti
1 tsp salt
two 200-g/7-oz tins tuna fish
1 large onion, finely chopped
1 garlic clove, finely chopped
one 400-g/14-oz tin tomatoes in juice
2 tbsp chopped thyme
8 black olives, stoned and quartered
1 tbsp grated Parmesan cheese

Break up the spaghetti and put into a dish. Cover with water and add the salt. Microwave on high for 10 minutes. Drain the spaghetti and rinse through with cold water. Drain again.

Pour the oil from the tuna fish, reserving 3 tbsp. Flake the fish. Put the onion into a dish with the garlic and reserved oil. Cover with cling-film or a lid and microwave on high for 4 minutes.

Finely chop the tomatoes and add to the dish, together with their juice. Add the spaghetti and thyme. Microwave on high, uncovered, for 5 minutes. Mix in the tuna fish and olives. Scatter the cheese over the top and microwave on high, uncovered, for a further 2 minutes. Serve straight from the dish.

SAUSAGE AND MUSHROOM PILAFF

1 large onion, quartered and thinly sliced
1 garlic clove, finely chopped
25g/1 oz butter
600ml/1 pint ham stock, boiling
2 tsp ground turmeric
225g/8 oz long grain brown rice
one 200-g/7-oz boiling sausage
225g/8 oz mushrooms
1 large green pepper
4 tbsp chopped parsley

Put the onion, garlic and butter into a large bowl. Cover with cling-film or a lid and microwave on high for 4 minutes. Add the stock, turmeric and rice. Microwave, covered, on high for 15 minutes.

Meanwhile, halve the sausage lengthways and thinly slice. Thinly slice the mushrooms and cut the pepper into 2.5cm/1in strips. Mix these into the rice and microwave on high for a further 10 minutes.

Mix in the parsley and leave the pilaff to stand for 10 minutes before serving.

DESSERTS

Fruit-based desserts are easy to make in a micro-wave cooker as the fruit cooks so quickly. Even dried fruits can be cooked without having to be previously soaked.

Crumble toppings cook in minutes and sponge and suet puddings remain light and moist. Milk puddings will not brown in the cooker but if you like to have the skin on the top you can put them into an ovenproof dish and brown them under a conventional grill.

ALMOND STUFFED APPLES

4 large cooking apples
100g/4 oz almonds
2 tbsp honey
¼ tsp ground cloves
50g/2 oz raisins

Core the apples and score them round the middle. Blanch and grind the almonds. Mix the almonds with the honey and cloves. Finely chop the raisins and mix in well.

Fill the apples with the almond mixture and lay on a flat dish. Microwave on high for 8 minutes.

CINNAMON PEARS

675g/1½ lb firm pears
1 tsp ground cinnamon
200ml/7 fl oz dry red wine
2 tbsp honey
soured cream for serving

Peel and core the pears. Halve them crossways and cut into thin lengthways strips. Put the pear strips into a dish and toss in the cinnamon. Pour in the wine and add the honey.

Cover with cling-film or a lid and microwave on high for 10 minutes. Leave the pears for 2 minutes and then serve hot. Serve the soured cream separately.

BLACKBERRY FLUMMERY

675g/1½ lb blackberries
2 tbsp water
4 cloves
2 allspice berries
2 tbsp honey or sugar
2 tsp arrowroot

Put the blackberries into a bowl with the water, cloves and allspice. Cover with cling-film or a lid and microwave on high for 10 minutes so that the blackberries are soft and juicy. Rub through a sieve. Return to the cleaned bowl and microwave on high for 2 minutes to heat through. Add the honey or sugar and stir until it dissolves.

Put the arrowroot into a bowl and gradually stir in 6 tbsp of the blackberry purée to make a smooth paste. Gradually stir the paste back into the rest of the blackberry purée. Microwave on high for 3 minutes, stirring every 30 seconds. The mixture should be thick but transparent.

Pour into a serving bowl and leave in a cool place so the flummery becomes softly set.

PLUM BRULÉE

450g/1 lb plums
¼ tsp ground cinnamon
4 tbsp sherry
75g/3 oz demerara sugar
3 egg yolks
175ml/6 fl oz milk
150ml/¼ pint double cream

Halve and stone the plums. Put into an ovenproof dish and sprinkle with the cinnamon, sherry and 50g/2 oz of the sugar. Cover with cling-film and microwave on high for 2 minutes. Cool completely.

In a small bowl, beat together the egg yolks, milk and cream. Microwave on low for 6 minutes stirring every minute for the first 4 minutes and every 30 seconds thereafter. Cool completely.

Pour the cream sauce over the plums. Scatter the rest of the sugar over the top and microwave on high, uncovered, for 2 minutes.

STRAWBERRY CHEESECAKE

200g/7 oz plain wholewheat biscuits
75g/3 oz vegetable margarine
25g/1 oz Barbados sugar
1/4 tsp vanilla essence
350g/12 oz strawberries
15g/1/2 oz gelatine
juice of 1/2 lemon
2 tbsp water
50g/2 oz honey or caster sugar
175g/6 oz low-fat soft cheese

Put the biscuits in a polythene bag or between 2 pieces of greaseproof paper and crush to fine crumbs with a rolling pin. Put the vegetable margarine into a bowl. Microwave on high for 1 minute to melt. Mix in the biscuit crumbs, sugar and vanilla essence. Use the mixture to line the base and sides of a 25cm/10in flan dish. Microwave on high for 5 minutes.

Rub 225g/8oz of the strawberries through a sieve. Put the gelatine into a bowl with the lemon juice and water. Microwave the gelatine on high for 1 minute to melt. Stir in the honey (or caster sugar) and strawberry purée. Leave the mixture until it is on the point of setting. Using an electric beater, whip in the cheese.

Spread the cheese and strawberry filling over the pastry base. Leave in a cool place to set. Just before serving, decorate the top with the remaining strawberries.

ORANGE AND YOGHURT SOUFFLÉ

juice of 1 1/2 oranges and grated rind of 1 orange
15g/1/2 oz gelatine
2 tbsp water
50g/2 oz caster sugar
3 eggs, separated
200ml/7 fl oz natural yoghurt

Tie a double thickness of oiled greaseproof paper round a 12cm/4 1/2 in soufflé dish.

Put the gelatine into a bowl and stir in the water, sugar and egg yolks. Microwave on high for 1 minute, stirring after 30 seconds.

Beat the mixture with an electric beater until it is smooth and creamy. Beat in the orange rind and juice. Leave the mixture in a cool place until it is on the point of setting.

Whip the yoghurt into the setting mixture. Stiffly whip the egg whites and fold into the rest.

Pour the soufflé into the prepared dish and leave in a cool place to set. Remove the paper before serving.

APRICOT AND ORANGE COMPOTE

350g/12 oz whole dried apricots
450ml/¾ pint natural orange juice
5cm/2in cinnamon stick
2 tbsp orange liqueur
2 large oranges
cold water

Put the apricots into a bowl with the orange juice and cinnamon stick. Cover with cling-film or a lid and microwave on high for 12 minutes. Add the orange liqueur and leave the apricots for 30 minutes.

Meanwhile thinly pare the rind from the oranges. Put the rind into a bowl and cover with cold water. Microwave on high for 4 minutes. Drain. Cut the remaining pith from the oranges. Cut the oranges in half lengthways and thinly slice.

Add the oranges and peel to the apricots and chill the compote before serving.

CHOCOLATE BANANA CRUMBLE

6 bananas
grated rind and juice of 1 orange
100g/4 oz wholewheat flour
pinch of salt
50g/2 oz demerara sugar
50g/2 oz butter
50g/2 oz plain chocolate, grated
50g/2 oz chopped toasted hazelnuts

Slice the bananas and put into a pie dish with the orange rind and juice.

Put the flour, salt and sugar into a bowl and rub in the butter. Mix in the chocolate and hazelnuts. Cover the bananas with the crumble mixture and microwave on high for 8 minutes.

RICH SEMOLINA PUDDING

50g/2 oz wholewheat semolina
600ml/1 pint milk
75g/3 oz sultanas
25g/1 oz Barbados sugar
2 egg yolks

Put the semolina into a buttered 2.75 litre/5 pint bowl. Stir in the milk and add the sultanas and sugar. Cover with cling-film. Microwave on high for 6 minutes or until the milk is boiling. Stir. Reduce the heat to low and microwave for 10-15 minutes, stirring every 5 minutes until the pudding is thick and creamy.

Beat in the egg yolks, one at a time. Microwave on low for 2 minutes, stirring every 30 seconds. Transfer the pudding to an ovenproof dish.

Pre-heat the grill of a conventional cooker to high. Put the pudding under the grill for 7-8 minutes for a brown skin to form on the surface.

LAYERED APPLE AND GINGER PUDDING

175g/6 oz 85% wheatmeal flour
2 tsp baking powder
pinch of salt
75g/3 oz beef suet, freshly grated
4 pieces stem ginger, finely chopped
4 tbsp cold water
450g/1 lb cooking apples
2 tbsp syrup from the ginger jar
2 tbsp Barbados sugar

Mix together the flour, baking powder, salt, suet and stem ginger. Mix to a dough with the water.

Peel, core and chop the apples. Put into a bowl with the ginger syrup and sugar. Cover them with cling-film or a lid and microwave on high for 5 minutes.

Set aside one-third of the dough and divide the remaining piece into 3 equal parts. Roll out 1 piece to a size just bigger than the base of a 900ml/1½ pint pudding basin. Line the bottom of the greased basin with the circle of dough. Put in one-third of the apples, the next small piece of dough, rolled to a size just bigger than the first, another third of the apples and the final small piece of dough. Add the remaining apples and the reserved piece of dough, rolled out to fit the top of the basin.

Cover with cling-film or a lid and microwave on high for 10 minutes.

HONEY RING

100g/4 oz butter, plus extra for greasing
50g/2 oz Barbados sugar
175g/6 oz honey
175g/6 oz 85% wheatmeal self-raising flour
¼ nutmeg, grated
3 eggs, beaten
3 tbsp milk

Cream together the butter and sugar and two-thirds of the honey. Toss the flour with the nutmeg. Beat the flour into the butter, alternately with the eggs. Beat in the milk.

Grease a 20cm/8in ring mould and spoon the remaining honey evenly in the base. Spread the mixture over the honey.

Microwave on high for 6 minutes. Leave the pudding for 10 minutes before turning out.

WHOLEWHEAT CHRISTMAS PUDDING

50g/2 oz wholewheat flour
1 tsp baking powder
50g/2 oz fresh wholewheat breadcrumbs
50g/2 oz fresh beef suet, grated
50g/2 oz currants
50g/2 oz sultanas
50g/2 oz large raisins
40g/1½ oz almonds, blanched and chopped
25g/1 oz candied peel, finely chopped
25g/1 oz glacé cherries, quartered
1 tsp ground mixed spices
1 small carrot, finely grated
1 small dessert apple, finely grated
grated rind and juice of ½ orange
1 egg, beaten
6 tbsp brandy

Mix together all the dry ingredients. Add the orange juice, egg and brandy and mix well. Put the mixture into a greased 600ml/1 pint pudding basin. Cover with cling-film or a lid and microwave on high for 6 minutes.

The pudding may be eaten straight away or covered with aluminium foil for storing and reheated when required by microwaving on high for 2 minutes. Serves 4–6.

BAKING

Cakes and bread can be cooked quickly and successfully in a microwave oven. They taste delicious and their texture is good, but they will not brown. To overcome this, bread can be brushed with beaten egg and sprinkled with cracked wheat or poppy seeds before baking. Or you can finish it with a browning element or under a high grill on a conventional cooker.

Cakes can be sprinkled with chopped nuts or brown sugar towards the end of the cooking time, or they can be decorated when cool. Wholewheat or wheatmeal flour will also give good results.

When mixing cakes to be cooked in the microwave oven, make them with self-raising flour or, if you use plain flour with a raising agent, reduce the amount of raising agent by about a quarter as the cake cooks quickly and there will be no time for the flavour to cook out.

Cakes can be cooked in a variety of containers. As the microwaves can only penetrate the cake to a certain depth you may find that you would rather cook them in a ring mould since this will avoid the problem of having a rather moist centre. Large cakes can also be cooked in special microwave-proof cake moulds or in straight-sided soufflé dishes.

Never grease and flour the container as this will give an unattractive flour film on the outside. You can lightly grease the container or line it with cling-film or greaseproof paper. Only half-fill the container as microwaved cakes rise very high.

Small cakes are best cooked in paper cases which have been placed in a muffin container or into teacups to stop the cakes from spreading.

When they come out of the oven, the cakes will look soft and undercooked, but they will firm during the standing time. Do not put them back into the oven or they will overcook. Test cakes by inserting a fine skewer into the centre. When the cake is turned out it may have a small tacky area underneath. This often disappears once the cake has cooled. If not, put the cake under a hot grill.

Double crust pies cannot be cooked in a microwave as the food tends to cook before the pastry. Flaky, rough puff and hot water pastries are also not suitable for microwave ovens.

Open tarts and quiches can be cooked successfully in a microwave oven, provided the pastry has been baked blind first. To do this, line a china or special flan dish with pastry. Cover the base of the pastry with a double layer of kitchen paper and the edges with aluminium foil. Microwave on high for 4 minutes. Remove the paper and foil and microwave on high for a further 1–2 minutes, depending on the size of the dish.

APPLE CUSTARD TART

shortcrust pastry made with 175g/6 oz flour
350g/12 oz cooking apples
50g/2 oz honey
3 eggs, beaten
150ml/¼ pint milk
freshly grated nutmeg

Roll out the pastry thinly and use to line an 18cm/7in tart dish. Bake blind.

Peel, core and chop the apples and put into a dish with the honey. Cover and microwave on high for 5 minutes. Rub the apples through a sieve. Mix in the eggs and milk. Pour the apple mixture into the pastry case and sprinkle over a little nutmeg.

Microwave on low for 16 minutes. Leave the tart for 10 minutes before serving.

SMOKED MACKEREL QUICHE

shortcrust pastry made with 225g/8 oz
  85% wheatmeal flour
350g/12 oz smoked mackerel fillets
1 medium onion, thinly sliced
25g/1 oz butter
225g/8 oz tomatoes
4 eggs
1 tbsp tomato purée
2 tbsp chopped parsley
¼ tsp Tabasco sauce

Line a 25cm/10in tart dish with the pastry. Bake blind.

Skin, bone and flake the mackerel. Put the onion into a bowl with the butter. Cover with cling-film or a lid and microwave on high for 4 minutes. Cool.

Thinly slice the tomatoes and lay the slices in the pastry case. Beat the eggs with the tomato purée, parsley and Tabasco sauce. Stir in the onion and mackerel. Pour the mixture over the tomatoes, distributing it evenly.

Microwave on high for 10 minutes and leave the quiche to stand for 5 minutes before serving.

CUP CAKES

100g/4 oz vegetable margarine
50g/2 oz drinking chocolate
50g/2 oz Barbados sugar
100g/4 oz 85% wheatmeal flour
2 eggs, beaten
4 tbsp milk

Cream the margarine and beat in the drinking chocolate and sugar. Beat in the flour and the eggs in turn. Beat in the milk.

Half-fill 12 paper cake cases with the mixture. Arrange, 6 at a time, round the edge of a large, flat plate or a special muffin pan.

Microwave for 2 minutes and transfer to a wire rack to cool.

LEMON SPONGE CAKE

175g/6 oz butter
175g/6 oz light Barbados sugar
grated rind and juice of 1 lemon
175g/6 oz 85% wheatmeal self-raising flour
3 eggs, beaten
FILLING
225g/8 oz curd cheese
2 tbsp honey
grated rind of 1 lemon

Beat the butter to a cream. Beat in the sugar and lemon rind and then the flour in turn with the eggs. Beat in the lemon juice.

Put the mixture into a well-buttered 20cm/8in ring mould. Microwave on high for 8 minutes. Cool the cake for 5 minutes in the mould. Turn onto a wire rack to cool.

Beat the cheese with the honey and lemon rind. Cut the cake in half crossways. Spread the bottom half with about one-third of the cheese. Sandwich the halves back together and spread the cake with the remaining cheese.

CIDER GINGER CAKE

175g/6 oz 85% wheatmeal self-raising flour
1 tsp ground ginger
1 tsp bicarbonate of soda
75g/3 oz butter, softened
50g/2 oz Barbados sugar
25g/1 oz molasses
2 eggs, beaten
6 tbsp dry cider

Mix the flour with the ginger and soda. Cream the butter and beat in the sugar and molasses. Beat in the eggs and the flour in turn. Add the cider.

Put the mixture into a buttered 20cm/8in cake mould or dish. Microwave on high for 8 minutes. Leave the cake in the tin for 10 minutes before turning out.

RICH FRUIT CAKE

175g/6 oz butter
175g/6 oz Barbados sugar
2 tbsp molasses
225g/8 oz 85% wheatmeal self-raising flour
2 tsp ground mixed spice
3 eggs, beaten
2 tbsp dark rum (or milk)
225g/8 oz sultanas
225g/8 oz raisins
225g/8 oz currants
75g/3 oz glacé cherries, halved

Cream the butter and sugar together and beat in the molasses. Toss the flour with the mixed spice. Beat the flour into the butter, in turn with the eggs and rum (or milk). Fold in the dried fruits and cherries.

Put the mixture into a 20cm/8in straight-sided dish, lined with greaseproof paper. Stand the dish in the microwave on an upturned saucer or a small dish. Microwave on defrost for 45 minutes.

Leave the cake to stand for 30 minutes before turning onto a wire rack to cool completely.

CARAWAY AND RAISIN SCONES

225g/8 oz 85% wheatmeal flour
1 tsp salt
1 tsp bicarbonate of soda
40g/1½ oz butter
1 tsp caraway seeds
50g/2 oz raisins
150ml/¼ pint sour milk, buttermilk
   or natural yoghurt
50g/2 oz honey

Put the flour into a bowl with the salt and soda. Rub in the butter. Toss in the caraway seeds and raisins. Make a well in the centre. Pour in the milk (or buttermilk or natural yoghurt) and add the honey. Mix everything to a dough. Turn onto a floured work surface and knead lightly.

Roll out the dough to a thickness of 2cm/¾in. Stamp into 5cm/2in rounds with a pastry cutter. Put the rounds onto a flat dish and microwave on high for 6 minutes, changing the outside ones to the centre and the centre ones to the outside after 3 minutes.

Leave the scones for 10 minutes before lifting onto a wire rack to cool completely.

BACON AND CHEESE SCONES

100g/4 oz lean bacon rashers
75g/3 oz Cheddar cheese
225g/8 oz 85% wheatmeal flour
1 tsp salt
1 tsp bicarbonate of soda
40g/1½ oz lard
150ml/¼ pint sour milk, buttermilk
   or natural yoghurt

Put the bacon rashers onto a plate between 2 pieces of kitchen paper. Microwave on high for 2 minutes and finely chop the bacon. Grate the cheese.

Put the flour into a bowl with the salt and soda. Rub in the lard. Toss in the bacon and cheese. Pour in the sour milk (or buttermilk or yoghurt) and mix everything to a dough. Turn onto a floured work surface and knead lightly.

Roll out the dough to a thickness of 2cm/¾in and stamp into 5cm/2in rounds with a pastry cutter. Put the rounds on a flat dish and microwave on high for 6 minutes, changing the outside ones to the centre and the centre ones to the outside after 3 minutes.

Leave the scones for 10 minutes before lifting onto a wire rack to cool completely.

WHOLEWHEAT BREAD

450g/1 lb wholewheat flour, plus extra for
   kneading
2 tsp salt
25g/1 oz fresh or 15g/½ oz dried yeast
1 tsp honey or Barbados sugar
300ml/½ pint warm water
beaten egg for glaze

Put the flour and salt into a bowl. Cream the yeast
with the honey or sugar. Stir in half the water and
leave the yeast mixture in a warm place for about 10
minutes until it begins to froth.

Make a well in the flour. Pour in the yeast
mixture and the remaining water. Mix everything
to a dough. Turn the dough onto a floured work
surface and knead until smooth.

Press the dough lightly into an oiled bread mould
and brush with beaten egg. Cover with cling-film
or put into a roasting bag. Leave in a warm place for
1 hour or until doubled in size.

Uncover the loaf and microwave on high for 6
minutes. Leave the loaf in the mould for 10 minutes
and then turn onto a wire rack to cool.

QUICK HAM PIZZA

225g/8 oz 85% wheatmeal self-raising flour
½ tsp salt
50g/2 oz vegetable margarine
1 egg, beaten
6 tbsp milk
225g/8 oz tomatoes
1 medium onion, finely chopped
1 garlic clove, finely chopped
3 tbsp oil
1 tbsp chopped thyme
100g/4 oz ham, finely chopped
175g/6 oz Mozarella cheese
12 anchovy fillets
10 black olives

Put the flour and salt into a bowl. Rub in the
margarine. Make a well in the centre and add the
egg and milk. Mix everything to a dough. Roll out
to a diameter of 30cm/12in and use to line a 25cm/
10in flat dish, folding over the edges to thicken
them and make the dough fit.

Scald, skin and chop the tomatoes. Put the
onion, garlic and oil into a bowl. Cover with cling-
film or a lid and microwave on high for 4 minutes.
Mix in the tomatoes and thyme. Microwave on
high, uncovered, for 5 minutes. Mix in the ham.

Cover the pizza base with the ham mixture.
Thinly slice the cheese and lay on the top. Cut the
anchovy fillets in half lengthways. Halve and stone
the olives and arrange on top of the cheese. Microwave the pizza on high for 8 minutes.

SAUCES

Sauces can be cooked in the microwave oven in the same jug or dish in which they are going to be served – so saving on time and the washing-up.

Make sure the container is large enough in case the sauce boils up and, for the smoothest results, stir several times during cooking.

QUICK APPLE SAUCE

450g/1 lb cooking apples
15g/½ oz butter
¼ tsp ground cloves

Core and chop the apples. Put the chopped apples into a bowl, dot with butter and sprinkle with the ground cloves. Cover with cling-film or a lid and microwave on high for 10 minutes. Beat the apples to a purée and serve the sauce hot.

BASIC WHITE SAUCE

25g/1 oz butter
2 tbsp flour
300ml/½ pint milk
salt and pepper if required

Put the butter into a bowl and microwave on high for 30 seconds to melt. Stir in the flour and milk. Season to taste. Microwave on high for 4 minutes, stirring well at 2 minutes and again at the end of the cooking time.

Variations For parsley sauce, stir 4 tbsp chopped parsley into the finished sauce.

For caper sauce, add 1 tbsp chopped capers and 2 tbsp chopped parsley.

For mushroom sauce, microwave 75g/3 oz chopped button mushrooms with the butter, covered, for 2 minutes before stirring in the flour.

For onion sauce, microwave 1 chopped medium onion with the butter, covered, for 4 minutes before stirring in the flour.

For a tomato-flavoured sauce, stir 1 tbsp tomato purée into the butter with the flour; 1 tsp paprika and/or ¼ tsp cayenne pepper may also be added.

BARBEQUE SAUCE

450g/1 lb tomatoes
1 medium onion, finely chopped
2 tbsp malt vinegar
2 tbsp Worcestershire sauce
2 tbsp soy sauce
1 tbsp Barbados sugar

Finely chop the tomatoes and put into a bowl with the remaining ingredients. Microwave on high, uncovered, for 10 minutes.

Rub the mixture through a sieve or put through the fine blade of a vegetable mill. Return the purée to the bowl and microwave on high for 2 minutes.

TOMATO SAUCE

450g/1 lb tomatoes
1 small onion, finely chopped
2 tbsp malt vinegar
1 tsp salt
freshly ground black pepper
15g/½ oz butter
1 tbsp flour

Finely chop the tomatoes and put into a bowl with the onion, vinegar and salt and a liberal amount of black pepper. Microwave on high, uncovered, for 10 minutes. Put everything through the medium blade of a vegetable mill.

Put the butter into the cleaned bowl and microwave on high for 30 seconds to melt. Stir in the flour and the puréed tomato. Microwave on high for 4 minutes, stirring after the first 2 minutes.

HOLLANDAISE SAUCE

4 tbsp white wine vinegar
6 black peppercorns
1 blade mace
1 onion slice
1 bayleaf
150g/5 oz unsalted butter
3 egg yolks
1 tbsp single cream or top of the milk

Put the vinegar into a small bowl with the peppercorns, mace, onion slice and bayleaf. Microwave on high for 2 minutes and strain.

Put the butter into a bowl and microwave on high for 1½ minutes to melt. Beat the egg yolks in another bowl and gradually beat in 2 tbsp of the melted butter. Beat in all the vinegar mixture and then the remaining butter.

Microwave on high for 45 seconds, beating well after each 15 seconds. Beat in the cream or milk and serve as soon as possible.

CUMBERLAND SAUCE

3 large oranges
6 tbsp redcurrant jelly
1 tsp made English mustard
150ml/¼ pint port

Scrub the oranges. Thinly pare away the rinds and cut into matchstick-sized strips. Put the strips into a bowl, cover with cold water and microwave on high for 4 minutes. Drain.

Put the orange rind into a bowl with the redcurrant jelly and mustard. Beat with a fork to break up the jelly. Microwave on high for 3 minutes, stirring with a fork every 30 seconds.

Stir in the port and microwave on high for 2 minutes, stirring at 1 minute. Leave the sauce in a cool place for about 1 hour until cold and thick.

CHOCOLATE SAUCE

300ml/½ pint milk
15g/½ oz cornflour
25g/1 oz honey or sugar
50g/2 oz plain chocolate, chopped
15g/½ oz butter

In a bowl, mix 4 tbsp of the milk into the cornflour. Put the remaining milk into a jug with the honey or sugar and microwave on high for 4 minutes, stirring after 2 minutes to help the honey or sugar to dissolve.

Gradually stir the hot milk into the cornflour mixture. Microwave on high for 2 minutes, stirring at 30 seconds and at 1 minute. Stir in the chocolate and microwave on high for 1 minute more.

Beat in the butter, in small pieces, to give a glossy finish.

ORANGE SAUCE

300ml/½ pint natural orange juice
15g/½ oz cornflour
grated rind of ½ orange
1 tbsp orange liqueur (optional)

In a bowl, mix 4 tbsp of the orange juice into the cornflour. Put the remaining juice into a jug and microwave on high for 3 minutes.

Gradually stir the hot juice into the cornflour mixture. Microwave on high for 3 minutes, stirring at 30 seconds, 1 minute and 2 minutes.

Stir in the orange rind and the liqueur, if using.

CUSTARD SAUCE

300ml/½ pint creamy milk
1 vanilla pod or ¼ tsp vanilla essence
2 tbsp caster sugar
2 egg yolks

Put the milk into a jug with the vanilla pod (or essence). Microwave on low for 5 minutes. Remove the vanilla pod and stir in the sugar. Beat the egg yolks in a bowl and beat into the milk. Microwave on low for 6 minutes, stirring every minute.

PRESERVES

Sauces, chutneys, jams, jellies and marmalades can all be cooked in a microwave oven. They retain a good colour and flavour and require less attention than when cooked on a hob.

It is best to make preserves only in small amounts. Preserves should fill half- or one-third of the container, to prevent them from boiling up and spilling over. A large, heat-resistant bowl is the best cooking utensil.

The initial cooking of the fruit for jams is far quicker than by conventional methods, but it may take the same amount of time to reach the setting point. Test this by dropping a teaspoonful of the jam onto a cold plate or use a thermometer. Never leave a thermometer in the preserve unless it has been designed for use in a microwave oven.

SEVILLE ORANGE MARMALADE

900g/2 lb Seville oranges
1 lemon
1.2 litres/2 pints boiling water
1.8 kg/4 lb preserving sugar

Scrub the oranges and lemon and cut in half. Squeeze out the juice and remove the pips. Tie the pips in a piece of muslin.

If a marmalade with a more bitter flavour is required, leave the pith on the peel. For a milder flavour, scrape away the pith. Shred the peel, either coarsely or finely. Put the peel, juice and bag of pips into a bowl. Add 300ml/½ pint boiling water and leave for 1 hour. Remove the bag of pips, squeezing to extract the flavour. Add the remaining boiling water. Cover with cling-film and microwave on high for 20 minutes for thin cut, 30 minutes for thick cut.

Stir in the sugar and continue stirring until the sugar dissolves. Microwave on high, uncovered, for 45–50 minutes, or until setting point is reached, stirring every 10 minutes.

Allow the marmalade to stand for 30 minutes.

REDCURRANT JELLY

1.8kg/4 lb redcurrants
300ml/½ pint water
450g/1 lb sugar per 600ml/1 pint juice

Put the redcurrants into a large bowl with the water. Microwave on high, uncovered, for 15 minutes. Strain the currants in a jelly bag to extract the juice. Measure the juice and return to the cleaned bowl. Microwave on high for 4 minutes. Put the

required amount of sugar into a shallow dish. Microwave on high for 5 minutes to warm. Add the sugar to the hot juice and stir until the sugar dissolves.

Microwave on high for 45 minutes or until setting point is reached, stirring every 10 minutes.

When the jelly has cooled slightly, pour into jars and cover with rounds of greased paper. Cover completely when cool.

APPLE & DATE CHUTNEY

900g/2 lb cooking apples
675g/1½ lb stoned dates
450g/1 lb onions
100g/4 oz Barbados sugar
175g/6 oz molasses
1 tsp salt
1 tsp ground allspice
1 tsp cayenne pepper
600ml/1 pint white wine vinegar

Peel, core and finely chop the apples. Finely chop the dates and onions. Put all the ingredients into a large bowl and cover with a lid or cling-film.

Microwave on high for 10 minutes or until boiling. Stir. Cover again and microwave on high for 45 minutes or until thick, stirring after each 15

minutes. Cool the chutney slightly. Put into warm jars and immediately cover tightly.

TOMATO KETCHUP

1.5kg/3 lb ripe tomatoes
1 tbsp salt
175g/6 oz onions, finely chopped
200ml/7 fl oz malt vinegar
75g/3 oz demerara sugar
1 tsp ground black pepper
1 tsp ground cinnamon
½ tsp ground mace

Slice the tomatoes and place in layers in a large bowl with the salt. Leave for 2 hours.

Add the remaining ingredients. Microwave on high, uncovered, for 30 minutes.

Rub the mixture through the medium blade of a vegetable mill. Put the resulting purée into the cleaned bowl and microwave on high, uncovered, for 15 minutes or until it has thickened slightly.

Cool the ketchup and pour into bottles or jars. Cover tightly.

STRAWBERRY JAM

1.5kg/3 lb strawberries, hulled
juice of 1 lemon
1.5 kg/3 lb sugar

Put the strawberries into a large bowl with the lemon juice. Microwave on high, uncovered, for 15 minutes or until they are soft.

Stir in the sugar. Microwave on high, uncovered, for 40–50 minutes, or until setting point is reached, stirring after the first 10 minutes, then at 20 minutes, 30 minutes and then after every 5 minutes.

Allow the jam to cool slightly before covering with greased discs. Cover completely when the jam is cold.

HOT DRINKS

Making hot drinks in a microwave oven is quick and economical. You can heat one drink at a time or several together, and make them in the cup or container in which they are to be served. Never fill cups to the brim in case the liquid boils and spills. Always put several cups in a ring to ensure even heating.

MINT AND ORANGE TEA

FOR 2 DRINKS
1 tea bag
2 tbsp chopped fresh or 1 tbsp dried mint
juice of 1 orange
450ml/¾ pt water
2 slices of orange, halved

Put all the ingredients except the orange slices into a jug and microwave on high for 3 minutes. Leave the tea to brew for 2 minutes. Strain into cups or thick glasses and float an orange slice in each one.

CREAMY CARDAMON COFFEE

FOR 1 DRINK
150ml/¼ pint milk
150ml/¼ pint water
1 tbsp coffee essence
1 cardamon pod, crushed
1 tbsp whipped cream

Put the milk and water into a jug. Stir in the coffee essence and add the cardamon. Microwave on high for 3 minutes. Strain the coffee into a mug and float the cream on the top.

MARSHMALLOW CHOCOLATE

FOR 1 DRINK
300ml/½ pint milk
2.5cm/1in cinnamon stick
1 tbsp chocolate powder
2 marshmallows

Put the milk into a jug with the cinnamon stick and microwave on high for 2 minutes. Beat in the chocolate powder. Pour the drink into a mug and float the marshmallows on top. Microwave on high for 1 minute.

CIDER PUNCH

1 large orange
10 cloves
1 litre/1¾ pints dry cider
4 tbsp honey
10cm/4in cinnamon stick
150ml/¼ pint brandy

Stick the orange with the cloves and put on a plate. Microwave on high for 5 minutes. Thickly slice. Put the cider, sliced orange, honey and cinnamon stick into a large bowl. Microwave on high for 4 minutes. Add the brandy. Microwave on high for 30 seconds.

FLAKY MALTED MILK

FOR 1 DRINK
300ml/½ pint milk
2 tsp malted milk drink
1 large chocolate flake
1 tbsp whipped cream (optional)

Put the milk into a jug. Microwave on high for 2 minutes. Stir in the malted milk drink and pour the milk into a mug. Break off one-quarter of the flake and crumble over the milk. Microwave on high for 1 minute. Put the remaining piece of flake, whole, into the mug and float the cream on top if required.

MULLED RED WINE

1 large orange
1 lemon
24 cloves
1 bottle dry red wine
2 mace blades
10cm/4in cinnamon stick
75g/3 oz honey
1 crisp eating apple, cored, halved and thinly sliced

Stick the orange and lemon each with 12 cloves and put on a plate. Microwave on high for 5 minutes. Thickly slice. Put the wine into a bowl with the orange, lemon, mace, cinnamon and honey. Microwave on high for 3 minutes. Add the apple and microwave on high for 1 minute more.

HOT GROG

225ml/8 fl oz dark rum
225ml/8 fl oz still mineral water
3 tsp dark Barbados sugar
thick lemon slices, each stuck with 2 cloves
cm/2in cinnamon stick

Mix all the ingredients in a jug. Microwave on high for 2 minutes. Stir, pressing down on the lemon ces. Microwave on high for 1 minute. Pour the grog into warmed mugs or glasses.

HOT TODDY

225ml/8 fl oz whisky
225ml/8 fl oz still mineral water
juice of ½ lemon
1 tbsp honey, or more to taste
4 cloves
5cm/2in cinnamon stick

Mix all the ingredients in a jug. Microwave on high for 2 minutes. Stir and microwave on high for 1 minute. Pour the hot toddy into warmed mugs or glasses.

INDEX